Christopher Columbus

Admiral of the Ocean Sea

Christopher Columbus

Admiral of the Ocean Sea

Jim Haskins

SCHOLASTIC INC.
New York Toronto London Auckland Sydney

To Joseph

I am grateful to the Florida State Museum, the Institute for Early Contact Period Studies at the University of Florida, Kathy Benson, Ann Kalkhoff, and Louise Stephenson for their help on this book.

Photo Credits

Cover: Inset photo courtesy of the Library of Congress. Background photo courtesy of The Bettmann Archive. Insert: Photos 1, 4, 7, 10, and 14 courtesy of the Library of Congress. Photos 2, 3, 5, 6, 8, 9, 11, 12, 13, and 15 courtesy of The Bettmann Archive. Photo 16 courtesy of Wide World.

ISBN 0-590-42396-7

12 11 10 9 8 7 6 5 4 3 2   1 2 3 4 5/9

Printed in the U.S.A.   40

First Scholastic printing, October 1991

Contents

1
The Wool Weaver's Son

Christopher Columbus did not "discover" America. There were people living there already. They had probably arrived over land routes that existed between Asia and North America before the continents drifted apart thousands of years ago.

Columbus called the people he found "Indians" because he thought he had reached the Indies, which is what the people of Europe called Japan, China, India, and Indonesia. At that time, his first voyage in 1492, he did not know that the continents we call North and South America even existed. He thought that nothing lay between Europe and India and China but one huge ocean. He made three more voyages across that ocean, and on the third he realized that he had discovered a new continent. But he died believing he had reached the Indies.

During his lifetime, Christopher Columbus was not celebrated the way he is today. His great fame and all the honor that is paid to him occurred many years after he died. Today, we praise Christopher Columbus for doing something that he never intended to do and that he never even knew he had done.

Columbus was a brave explorer who set out into the unknown, sailing farther than anyone he knew about had ever sailed before. He did so at a time when there were no accurate maps of the world, much less any charts of currents in the Atlantic Ocean. Columbus was the first explorer in recorded history to cross the Atlantic Ocean. He was convinced he could reach India and China by sailing west, and he had the courage to act on his beliefs. While he was wrong in these beliefs, he gave the people of Europe more knowledge than they'd ever had before about what lay beyond the western coast of Europe. The sea route he established was basically followed by every explorer who came after him, and many of the lands he discovered still carry the names he gave them. These include the islands of the West Indies. They are nowhere near India and China, but because of the force of Columbus's beliefs they have been called the Indies ever since 1492.

Christopher Columbus was born in Italy about five hundred years ago. No one knows for certain the exact date, but it was sometime between August 25 and October 31, 1451. His parents were

Domenico and Susanna Fontanarossa Colombo. They may have had other children, for in those days many babies died in infancy, but Christopher was the first one who lived.

His parents named him Cristoforo. (His real name was Cristoforo Colombo, but since we know him by the English version of his name, we will call him Christopher Columbus here.) Like most Italians in those days, his parents were very religious, and they named him after Saint Christopher. Saint Christopher just happens to be the patron saint, or protector, of travelers. Since little Christopher grew up to be one of the most famous travelers in history, it is fitting that he was named after that particular saint.

Christopher's parents both came from families of weavers. Susanna Colombo was the daughter of a weaver. Domenico Colombo had a wool-weaving business. He owned looms and hired weavers to help him make wool cloth. He expected his children to help him in this business when they were old enough.

Of the four Columbus children who lived, three were boys and one was a girl. Christopher and Bartholomew were one or two years apart. The girl, Bianchetta, was fairly close in age to them. The third boy, Giacomo, better known as Diego, was seventeen years younger than Christopher.

The Columbus family lived in Genoa, an Italian seaport on the Mediterranean Sea. It was a large, busy city, and there was a big market for wool cloth to clothe all the people who lived there. Plus,

3

there were many other opportunities to make money in Genoa. Historians who have studied the life of Columbus say that his father tried getting into other kinds of businesses besides weaving. He wanted to make more money. But none of these attempts worked out, and he lost more than he made. Still, by the standards of the time, Christopher's family lived in a comfortable manner. They never went hungry and always had a roof over their heads and clothes for their bodies. Christopher and the other children did not go to school. In those days only the children of the rich had formal schooling. But Christopher did learn how to read and write when he was older.

We know that he had red hair and blue eyes. He probably had freckles when he was a child. He had a long face and a large, long nose that some people describe as beaked like a bird's. His fair skin reddened easily in the sun and wind and probably also when he was excited or embarrassed.

He was very close to his family. As a grown-up, he went into business with his brothers. He was also very religious. He named the islands he found after saints and said his prayers several times a day.

But he did not want to go into the wool-weaving business. He wanted to be a sailor.

There were certainly more sailors than wool weavers in Genoa in those days. In that busy port city everyone who didn't have some other kind of job was a sailor, or a dock worker, or had something to do with shipping. The business of Genoa revolved around shipping, from building ships to making sails to drawing maps to loading and un-loading cargo. Even those who were not directly involved in shipping found that their lives revolved around the sea and the weather. A period of calm with no wind meant that the ships did not sail into or out of the harbor. A stormy time meant ship-wrecks and the loss of lives. In each case, the city of Genoa was affected.

Besides bread, fish was a big part of everyone's diet in Genoa. Most people went fishing. They ate the fresh fish, but most who fished for a living dried some of their catch and then sold it. Dried and salted fish was a big part of the diet of people who did not live near the sea, and this was true all over Europe.

Christopher Columbus probably went fishing often when he was a small boy. And like children before and after, he must have wondered about the sea and what it would be like to set sail on a ship out into what seemed like a vast ocean. There is something exciting and forbidding about the sea. The waves roll in one after another, all day, every day. Watching them, one thinks about time, and about how the waves have been rolling in and rolling out long before we were born.

Genoese sailors all had their tales of adventure at sea, of battling great storms, of long periods with no wind, of shipwrecks, and pirate attacks. They told of strange and exotic ports in other lands, where the native peoples lived and spoke and dressed so differently. What visions their tales must have conjured up in a small boy's head! And how eager Christopher Columbus was to go to sea himself someday.

Christopher went to sea for the first time in 1461, when he was ten years old. It is likely that he went out to fish with a friend of the family, or on a short trip to a neighboring port to load cargo. Whatever kind of trip it was, it had a big impact on young Christopher. From then on, he was determined to be a sailor.

In those times, very young boys would go to sea. But they were orphans, or boys who were so poor that their families could not take care of them. They went to sea as apprentice seamen. They would work on the ships, and in return they would be fed and clothed and taught a seaman's trade. Some were cabin boys, whose job it was to tidy up the cabins and run errands for the ship's officers. Others had the job of turning the half-hourglass when the sands ran through. Other boys helped mend sails, serve food to the officers and sailors, and light the ship's lanterns at night.

When he was young, Christopher may have envied these boys, but when he grew older, he understood that they could never hope to be captain of a ship. They would only be regular sailors. Because Christopher was born to a higher-class family, he didn't *need* to go to sea. He could *choose* to go. *And*, he could be a captain some day.

As the eldest son, Christopher was expected to take over his father's business one day. His younger brother, Bartholomew, did not have that same responsibility. So Bartholomew left Genoa and went to Lisbon, Portugal, where he got a job in a chart-making shop, where maps and navigational charts were drawn for sea captains.

While Christopher was a dutiful son and continued to work in his father's business, he also managed to go to sea. From his middle teens to his early twenties, he must have gone on several sea voyages. He talked later of a trading voyage to the island of Chios in the Aegean Sea. This voyage took him east all the way around the bottom tip of Greece and up almost to the mainland of Turkey.

When we speak here of statements Christopher made, we are referring to the few sources from his time that still exist. One is a book entitled *History of the Indies*, by Bartolome de los Casas, a priest and historian who lived in Christopher's time and who used excerpts from a journal of Christopher's first voyage that has since been lost. Another source is a biography written by Christopher's son, Ferdinand.

According to these writings, Christopher also said that at the age of nineteen he served in the war fleet of King Rene II of Anjou, who was then at war with the King of Aragon. He would not have been able to be part of either of these voyages if he hadn't had quite a bit of experience at sea.

In 1476, when he was twenty-five years old, Christopher was chosen as a foremast hand (meaning that he worked on the part of the ship in front of the main mast) on an armed convoy carrying a valuable cargo from Genoa to northern

Europe. Christopher sailed on a Flemish ship named *Bechalla*.

On the morning of August 13, 1476, a French fleet attacked the convoy off the southern coast of Portugal. The two fleets engaged in a mighty battle, and by evening four French ships and three from the Genoese convoy had gone down. *Bechalla*, the ship Christopher was on, was one of the Genoese ships that was sunk. Christopher, who was wounded in the battle, found himself in the sea. He managed to grasp onto a floating piece of wood. Using it as a life raft, he kicked for hours until he reached shore six miles away. He landed near the Portuguese port of Lagos. There, the local people found him and cared for him until he recovered from his battle wounds and his long ordeal in the water.

While he was at Lagos, Christopher told the people that he had a younger brother in Lisbon. As soon as he could travel, they sent him there.

2
Master Mariner

Bartholomew Columbus managed to get his older brother, Christopher, a job in the chart-making shop where he worked in Lisbon. How much time elapsed between Christopher's arrival and his employment in the shop is not known. We do know that he learned to read and write in Portugal and that those skills were very important in the chart-making business. He had to be able to read ships' logs and to make maps based on the latest information brought back by navigators.

Lisbon, the capital of Portugal, was a much larger city than Genoa. It was a city where education was stressed, and where there were many books to read. Christopher learned Latin and other languages, and in the chart-making shop he learned more about navigation and how to draw maps.

At that time, Lisbon was also the center of world exploration and discovery. The main reason for this was the interest of a Portuguese prince, Henry the Navigator. Henry had financed voyages out into the Atlantic and down along the west coast of Africa, the continent to the south of Portugal. He had been especially interested in the idea of sailing around Africa. No European had ever done that, and Henry sent many ships south to explore the African coast and try to reach the southern end of the continent.

In the course of these explorations, the Portuguese had begun to trade with Africans. They had also started the European slave trade. The first shipment of African slaves, captured by the Portuguese at the mouth of the Senegal River near what the Portuguese called Cape Verde (Green Cape), probably arrived in Lisbon in the 1430s.

Prince Henry had also established a center for collecting all that was known about the world and the sea. Every time a European navigator discovered a new island or some new knowledge about the sea, this office found out about it and recorded it.

Henry was curious to know more about the outside world. But he also was anxious to find sea routes to India and China and Japan. In those places, there was gold, silk cloth, and spices. Europeans had known about all these riches of the East since Marco Polo, an Italian like Columbus, had journeyed overland to the East in the late 1200s.

Marco Polo had brought back silks, spices, gold, and a variety of other things from China. These included window and door coverings made of thin slats of bamboo. Venetian craftsmen started making them and exporting them to other parts of Europe, where they became known as Venetian blinds.

Europeans could not get enough of these exotic things. They were especially interested in the spices from the East, because these spices did wonders for their food. In an age without refrigeration, a large part of people's diet was dried and salted meat and fish. The spices from the East gave Europeans a much greater variety of tastes. But they also wanted the silks and gold and were willing to pay high prices for them. European merchants started going overland to India and China to trade for these items, bringing them back, and selling them for a large profit.

All went well until the Muslim Seljug Turks captured the Holy Land. Since the 600s, the Turks, out of Central Asia, had been moving west, capturing territory as they went. In 1453 the captured city of Constantinople (now called Istanbul) was the major port from which goods brought overland from India and China were distributed to Europe. Blocked from reaching the East by land, Europeans started looking for sea routes to the East. This search led them to travel farther and farther down the west coast of Africa. But so far, no one had managed to round the southern tip of the African continent.

All this travel along the west coast of Africa produced new discoveries and new trading centers. But it hardly seemed the ideal solution to the problem of reaching India and China. The journey by sea around Africa was long and dangerous. Portuguese navigators had already tried nearly twenty times to do it; none had been successful. More than one navigator was convinced there must be an easier way. At Lisbon, the center of information on navigation, it was felt likely that some day an easier way might be found.

By this time, most educated people realized that the earth was round, not flat as some had believed in earlier times. They did not know, however, how to draw maps that took into account the global shape of the earth. They also didn't know very much about the world, compared to what we know today. Every new bit of geographical knowledge was important, especially to sailors and mapmakers.

Christopher and Bartholomew interviewed as many captains and sailors as they could to find out more information. Mariners were always coming into the port of Lisbon from journeys to Africa and to the Azores, a group of islands in the Atlantic due west of Lisbon. The Columbus brothers would invite them out for a meal and wine and ask them questions. They would take notes on the mariners' stories, and copy down the rough sketches that the mariners drew and compare these to their own maps.

Meanwhile, Christopher also continued to get firsthand experience at sea. In late 1476, the same year that he arrived in Lisbon, he signed on with a Portuguese ship that sailed to Belgium, Germany, Great Britain, and Ireland. In Ireland, he would have heard the legends of Iargalon, "the land beyond the sunset." He probably also heard the tales of St. Brendan, the Irish monk who was supposed to have set sail in a leather boat and traveled to unknown places in the Atlantic Ocean between 565 and 573.

Soon after returning from that voyage, Columbus shipped out again, this time to Iceland. Fortunately for him, the captain of the ship was not just a trader but an explorer as well. While near Iceland, the captain decided to do some exploring to the north and sailed to the edge of the Arctic Circle before heading back to Lisbon. This was an exciting detour for the young sailor and chart maker from Genoa.

Columbus had a great curiosity and was trained to ask questions and take notes. At every port he would have heard, perhaps for the first time, legends of navigation told by sailors from the North.

When Columbus was in Iceland, in February and March, 1477, voyages were probably still being made to and from Greenland and the land beyond. Records in Iceland mention such trips between 1362 and 1408, but they most certainly continued after this time. In 1432, Norway had declared that only the Norwegian Crown could trade with Greenland, but that was not likely to stop traders from other countries from going there.

With each voyage, Christopher became more and more knowledgeable about navigation and the nature of the world. In fact, the Columbus brothers became so skilled at making maps based on the latest geographical knowledge that they soon set up their own business, Columbus Brothers, Chart makers and Booksellers. In a thriving port like Lisbon, ships' pilots would seek as many charts as they could, in order to ensure a safer and more successful voyage.

It is likely that Bartholomew had the greater responsibility for the day-to-day running of the business, because Christopher went on more voyages. The year following his trip to the Arctic Circle, he was on a ship sailing to Madeira, off the coast of Morocco, to buy sugar.

Not long after he returned from Genoa to Lisbon, twenty-nine-year-old Christopher married Doña Felipa Perestrello e Moniz, the daughter of an important family in Portugal. Her father had been a well-known sea captain and explorer named Bartholomew Perestrello. Perestrello had been one of the discoverers of the island of Madeira. He had also made voyages down the west coast of Africa. He had kept journals and sea charts, and Columbus's new mother-in-law gave them to him to study. It is not known what was in these journals and charts, but they may have included legends about African exploration of lands far to the west.

When Bartholomew Perestrello was active in exploration, Africa south of the Sahara desert was an area about which Europeans knew very little. But it did not take the Portuguese explorers long to realize that there was much to be learned from sub-Saharan Africans, who had a highly civilized and developed culture when the Portuguese first arrived.

Of great interest were the tales told by African mariners, probably including stories about voyages to the West. According to an account published in Cairo, Egypt, in 1342, less than two centuries earlier the emperor of the Kingdom of Mali had sent two hundred ships into the west, telling them not to return until they had reached the end of the ocean. Only one ship came back to tell the story. The captain of that vessel reported that the ships had found a strong current flowing in the open sea, and that each had disappeared after entering it. His had been the last ship, and after the disappearance of all the others, he had decided not to enter the current but instead to turn around and go home.

There may also have been legends of much earlier voyages and discoveries in the West by Africans. We know now that there is evidence of the presence of black men in ancient Mexico and other parts of Central America, as well as in the Andes Mountains of South America. This evidence — statues and murals of black men, bits of African languages, and the presence of plants that are na-

tive to Africa, like the bottle gourd and cotton —
dates back more than a thousand years before Columbus. Definite knowledge of the lands we call
the Americas may have been lost by Columbus's
time, but legends may have stayed alive.

Perhaps Columbus read of some of these legends in the journals of his late father-in-law, Bartholomew Perestrello. He may have heard them
from some of the Senegalese slaves in Portugal.
There is no way to know exactly how he might
have learned of them. But based on the ideas he
would have later, he must have had some knowledge of these legends.

After living for a time in Lisbon, Christopher
Columbus and his wife moved to Porto Santo,
where Doña Felipa's brother was governor. Their
only child, Diego, was born there.

Later, they moved to the port of Funchal in Madeira, and while there Columbus made a couple
of voyages sponsored by the Portuguese merchant
service to St. George at El Mina, a new Portuguese
trading post on the Gold Coast of Africa (present-
day Ghana). On one of the voyages, he was in
command of a ship, which means he was considered a first-class pilot and navigator.

By this time he was in a position to make a great
deal of money through trade in Africa and the
Azores. He had the skills, and he had the power
and influence of a respected family. But Christopher Columbus had bigger plans. He wanted to
make a voyage west.

3
Columbus's Plan

Columbus wanted to make a voyage to the Indies, which is what Europeans of the time called everything from India to China to Japan to Indonesia. If he could make a successful voyage and bring back silks and spices, gold and precious stones from the Indies, he could make a fortune. He would also gain great fame as a navigator.

Deeply religious, he probably also wanted to see if he could help Christians regain the Holy Land from the Turks. It was believed that there was a powerful Christian state somewhere east of Persia and Armenia, which was ruled by a man named Presbyter John, or Prester John. Many Europeans believed that if they could join forces with Prester John, who was supposed to be very rich and powerful, they might be able to launch a successful war against the Turks.

Columbus's dreams depended upon the possibility of his finding a safe passage to the Indies. Many mariners believed that such a route existed. Based on the latest knowledge of the world and navigation, they believed that they could reach the Indies by sailing west, across the Ocean Sea.

They knew that the earth was round. Therefore, one would eventually reach the East by sailing west. The only problem was, no one knew how far around the earth was, and how long it would take to reach the East.

They had no idea that the continents now called North and South America even existed. They didn't realize there were two great oceans, not one. They may have heard rumors that four hundred years earlier the Norsemen of northern Europe had traveled across the northern Atlantic and reached the east coast of North America. However, it was generally believed that the world, consisting of Europe, Asia, and Africa, was like one big island in one huge Ocean Sea.

Columbus believed that he knew all the continents. He also believed that he had a pretty good idea of the size of the earth. Astronomers, mathematicians, and geographers had come up with a calculation based on the fact that there are 360 degrees in a circle. If they could figure out the length of one degree in nautical miles (one nautical mile equals about 2,000 yards), then they could also estimate the circumference of the earth. Popular guesses of the length of one degree ranged from forty-five to sixty-six nautical miles. Columbus liked the low estimate.

Different authorities, including Marco Polo, who had taken two or three years to cross Asia by land, estimated the size of the known major land mass, the huge "island" of Europe, Asia, and Africa. They guessed that the "island" took up a major portion of the earth. The guesses varied. Columbus believed the estimate that land covered six sevenths of the globe, and that the Ocean Sea took up only one seventh of the earth. Based on their estimates, Columbus calculated that if he started west from the Canary Islands, he would only have to sail 2,400 nautical miles before he reached the eastern shore of the continent.

Columbus was a young man with big dreams. It was natural for him to accept the idea that it wouldn't be so hard to sail westward and reach Japan. He wanted to do it. But in truth, what he believed was all wrong. A degree equals sixty nautical miles. Europe, Asia, and Africa take up only about one third of the earth. The distance between the Canary Islands and Japan is 10,600 miles. *And*, the American continents just happen to be in the way.

It took a great deal of money to finance a voyage of trade and exploration such as Christopher Columbus dreamed about.

He needed ships. He needed to hire seamen to sail those ships. Those seamen had to eat, and so all the ships had to be provisioned with food and water and wine. There had to be a ship's surgeon to care for the sailors when they became sick or injured. And, equally important, he needed to have a large supply of goods to trade with the local people in exchange for gold and spices and precious stones.

In Europe in those days, no one had that kind of money to risk but kings and queens and princes. And so Christopher Columbus set about trying to interest a member of royalty in his dream. He gathered up all the evidence he could find to support his theories about the size of the earth and the number of miles he thought lay between Europe and the Indies.

The first person Columbus approached was John II, King of Portugal. The king was a nephew of Henry the Navigator and himself very interested in exploration and discovery. But according to historical records, the king didn't think much of Columbus or his plan. He thought Columbus was "a big talker and boastful." The king's scientific advisers told him that Columbus's estimates of the distance to Japan were all wrong.

In the same year that the Portuguese king turned him down, Columbus's wife, Doña Felipa, died. That year, 1485, was a difficult one for Columbus. He left Portugal and the memories of his wife and the rejection he had suffered from the king.

With his son, Diego, Columbus crossed the border between Portugal and Spain and arrived in the area of Niebla. Columbus was not sure what to do with his little boy. He learned that there was a Franciscan monastery nearby, and he walked there with Diego. They were met at the monastery gate by a monk who just happened to be interested in astronomy. The monk invited both father and son to stay and accepted Diego as a student.

The monk, Antonio de Marchena, shared Columbus's interest in a voyage to Japan and introduced him to the Count of Medina Celi. The count was about to agree to support Columbus's voyage when he decided he had better ask the Queen of Spain for her permission. Queen Isabella felt that a voyage so important should be conducted in the name of the Crown. Unfortunately, she was in no hurry about it.

While Columbus waited to hear from the queen, he went to the nearby city of Cordova. There, he met a twenty-year-old girl named Beatriz Enriquez. In 1488, Beatriz bore him a son, whom they named Ferdinand, but Christopher never married Beatriz. She was a peasant's daughter and so she was not a suitable wife for someone of Christopher's class. Christopher took over the care of Ferdinand after a few years. Many years after that, when Christopher died, he left money for Beatriz's support.

It took Columbus nearly a year just to see the queen. She was close to him in age and also similar in physical appearance, with red hair and blue eyes. They probably liked each other. But that did not mean Isabella was ready to give Columbus the go-ahead. She appointed a special commission to study his plan.

The commission could not come to an agreement. Its members voted to give Columbus money to live on while they discussed the matter, but as the months wore on, Columbus became impatient. In late 1488 he returned to Lisbon to try again to interest the King of Portugal in his voyage. He was there in December when Bartholomew Diaz, the Portuguese navigator, returned in triumph from what was probably the twentieth Portuguese attempt to round the southern tip of Africa.

Diaz had rounded the south cape, which he had named the Cape of Good Hope. He had then started up the east coast of Africa, excited and filled with the "good hope" that he could reach the Indies. Unfortunately, after more than seven months, his men were sick of being at sea. They mutinied and forced him to turn back. But Diaz was still a hero and eager to try again. And the King of Portugal, knowing now that it was possible to reach the other side of Africa by sea, lost all interest in the idea of sailing west to accomplish the same thing.

Christopher stayed with his younger brother, Bartholomew, while he was in Lisbon. He convinced Bartholomew that he was right, and not long after the return of Diaz, the Columbus brothers decided to work together to get backing for the western voyage. While Christopher returned to Spain, Bartholomew closed up the chart-making business and traveled to other European capitals to try to interest other royalty in the enterprise. He went first to England, and when Henry VII wasn't interested, he proceeded to France. There, he became friendly with the sister of King Charles VIII and drew maps for her while hoping to interest her brother.

Back in Spain, Christopher settled for a time in the port of Seville and opened a branch of Columbus Brothers, Chart makers and Booksellers. He continued to wait for the queen's commission to come to a decision on his voyage. The commission finally issued its report late in 1490: Columbus's project was "impossible"; it would take far longer than he supposed; the ocean was much larger than he estimated.

Columbus despaired. He believed he had made very modest requests — only covering expenses. In his opinion, the Spanish court was passing up a rare bargain that would have brought it great wealth and influence. Queen Isabella tried to make him feel better by telling him he could try again. But he could see no point in it. He decided to join his brother in France. On the way, he picked up his son, Diego, who was now about ten years old. He told Father Juan Perez, the prior of the monastery, about his rejection by the queen's commission, and the prior urged him not to give up. Father Perez wrote to the queen, and Isabella, feeling sorry for Columbus, sent him money to buy some new clothing and a mule.

Around Christmas of 1491, Columbus applied a second time to the queen to support his voyage. This time his requests were far more ambitious. Not only did he want his voyage financed, he wanted wealth and honors if he made any important discoveries. He wanted to be given the title of admiral, to be named governor of any new lands he might discover, and to be given a ten percent share of any trade in which he engaged. Isabella appointed a new commission. This commission took very little time to reject the idea. King Ferdinand, Isabella's husband, told Columbus that the decision was final.

Dejected, Columbus packed up and started for Seville. There, he would close up his business and set off for France to join Bartholomew and pursue his project with King Charles VIII. Then, suddenly, Queen Isabella had a change of heart.

The reason probably had to do with two things. One was that Spain's long and costly war with the Moors was finally over. During the long war, the Spanish royalty had not had much money left over to spend on things like voyages of exploration. The other was the triumph of Bartholomew Diaz of Portugal. If a Portuguese sailor had found a way around Africa, then Portugal was going to have first shot at trade with the Indies by eastern routes. Portugal was already far ahead of Spain in navigation, exploration, and trade. Spain needed to start investing more money in finding new routes to the East that it could claim as its own. Where better to start than with a voyage by Christopher Columbus?

Queen Isabella sent a messenger after Columbus to bring him back. When he returned to court, he heard the news he had been hoping to hear for years. He could make his voyage to the Indies!

It took three more months to sign all the contracts the king and queen had drawn up. These were the terms that Columbus and the royal couple agreed to: Columbus would receive all the titles he asked for, and the ten percent he had requested of all gold, gems, spices, and other goods obtained by trade. When he died, he could pass on these benefits to his family. The king and queen agreed to provide him with three ships and the money needed to outfit them, load them with provisions, and hire men to sail them. They also provided him with three letters of introduction.

One of these letters was addressed to the "Grand Khan," which is the name by which Europeans knew the Chinese emperor. The other two had blank spaces where names should be, because no one knew what other rulers Columbus might meet. When he met someone he felt should get a royal letter of introduction, he could fill in the name.

Christopher Columbus had his financial backing at last. It had taken him many years to secure it. But he put aside all the despair and frustration now that he could finally get on with his dream.

As soon as possible, he went to Palos, the small port where he had first arrived in Spain. He had friends there, the Pinzons, who were shipbuilders and master mariners. There he acquired three ships that in the language of the sea are called "caravels." The name comes from the term *carvel*, which refers to the method of building. These were small ships, generally with three masts. It is said that one reason why Portugal took the lead in exploring the African coast was because of the development of these ships, which were less bulky than those used in other parts of Europe.

As his flagship, the lead vessel, Columbus chose the *Santa María*. The two smaller ships also carried the names of saints, which was the Spanish custom. One was the *Santa Clara*. The official name of the other is not known. Both were better known by their nicknames, the *Niña*, which means little girl, and the *Pinta*, which was probably named after a former owner named Pinto.

The *Santa María* and the *Pinta* were square-riggers, which means that they carried square sails. *Niña* was lateen-rigged with a triangular sail extended by a long spar attached to a short mast. Sails at that time, even when brand-new, were a brownish color because they were woven of flax. Not until cotton, which originated in Africa and was grown widely there and in the New World, was imported would Europeans be able to produce sails that were a glistening white when new.

All the sails were decorated with crosses and symbols. The parts of the wooden ships above the waterline were painted bright colors. Below the waterline, they were painted with pitch so as to keep barnacles and shipworms called *teredos* away. *Teredos* could grow to several feet long and as thick as a human arm. They could do terrible damage to wooden ships. At sea during periods of little or no wind, when the ships were hardly moving, barnacles and shipworms would soon cover the parts of the ship below the waterline and eat into the wood.

Each ship carried the royal flag of Queen Isabella with its lions and castles, and each ship also carried the special banner of the expedition, a white background with a green cross, a crown on each arm of the cross.

None of the ships had many weapons. All had enough to fight back against pirates, but none was a battleship. Columbus hired no soldiers. He did not expect to need them, for the Portuguese had never had much trouble with the local people in Africa, and he did not feel he would have problems with the people he would find in the Indies.

The men he did hire included the best captains and navigators he could find. There is some speculation that one of the navigators was black, but no one knows for sure. He might have been from the area around Senegal in western Africa, or from northern Africa in the area we now call Morocco.

Columbus also hired a surgeon, or doctor, for each ship. Each ship had a steward, who supervised the cooking and serving of food. There was a tailor, who would repair the men's clothing, and a cooper, who was an expert at making and repairing the barrels in which so much of the food and liquid were kept. Then, there were the boatswains, who were in charge of keeping the ships seaworthy; the caulkers, who kept the ships watertight; the ship's boys; and all the seamen needed to sail a ship.

Finally, there were several men whose jobs were especially important on such a voyage. One was responsible for keeping track of all the gold and other riches, to make sure the king and queen got their fair share. Another, named Luis de Torres, happened to know Arabic, a language people knew was spoken in the East, so Columbus decided he ought to be able to understand the Chinese and Japanese they would meet. Still another was the secretary of the fleet, who would make an official record of all the discoveries. Altogether, there were about ninety men, nearly all of them from the area of Palos. Each had great courage to embark on the venture, as well as his own dreams of wealth and fame.

Columbus, and everyone else, planned to bring back from the Indies far more than they carried with them. So when the ships were loaded there was a lot of space left over.

We do not know exactly what was loaded onto each ship for that particular voyage. If records exist, they have yet to be found. But based on records of other voyages, we know that a lot had to be taken to feed the men on a voyage whose length was anybody's guess.

Casks of water and wine were loaded onto the ships. So were tons of wheat, flour, sea biscuits, cheese, salt pork, olive oil, sardines, and garlic. Just before sailing, all sorts of livestock were herded aboard — hogs, sheep, goats, chickens, geese, and ducks. The ships had to carry live animals because that was the only way to get fresh food.

Goods for trade were also loaded onto the three ships. These included the items that Africans liked: red caps, glass beads, and hawks' bells — tiny bells that in Europe were used in the sport of falconry.

The rest of the space on the ships was filled with ballast: stones. These stones were needed to steady the ship. Columbus had every intention of leaving all those ballast stones on the shores of the Indies. In their place, he planned to return from the voyage with a cargo of equal weight but far greater value: gold and gems and spices.

4
Out into the Ocean Sea

The night before the small fleet was to set sail, everyone who was to make the journey went to the church of Palos, confessed their sins, and took communion. They firmly believed that God, Jesus, the Virgin Mary, and saints like Saint Christopher would protect those who were faithful to them. They certainly felt they needed divine protection, because they were sailing out into the unknown. Even Christopher Columbus, captain general of the fleet, must have had some moments of fear as he set out at last on the voyage he had dreamed about for so long.

Columbus's original journal from his first voyage is lost. When he returned, he gave it to Ferdinand and Isabella, and at least one copy was made. But neither the original nor the copy is known to exist now. As mentioned earlier, a priest and historian named Bartolome de los Casas later wrote a book called *History of the Indies*, in which he quoted from Columbus's journal. Columbus's younger son, Ferdinand, wrote a biography of his father, and he also included portions from the original journal. People who study the first voyage of Columbus have only these books as references.

Before dawn on the morning of August 3, 1492, the three ships weighed anchor and floated down the Tinto River on the morning tide. On that same tide traveled the *Saltes,* the last ship carrying the Jews that Ferdinand and Isabella had expelled from Spain. If Columbus was aware of this coincidence, it mattered little to him. As a staunch Christian, he would have supported the expulsion of the Jews from Spain. He already had decided that the colonies he would set up in the Indies would not allow Jews in.

Once they reached the Ocean Sea (the Atlantic Ocean), they headed south, taking advantage of the winds from the north, which caught the sails and built their speed.

It was Columbus's plan to sail first to the Canary Islands, then to begin the westward voyage. His reasons were several and sound. His experience on earlier voyages was that the sea was calm around the Canaries at that time of year. It was much easier to navigate there than in the stormy northern parts of the Ocean Sea. Also, the Canaries were located at the latitude of 28 degrees north. This was the same latitude at which Columbus thought Japan was located. He also believed that the legendary Isle of Antilia was on this latitude, and that if he sailed due west from the Canaries, he would reach it and be able to rest and take on supplies there.

It took less than a week to reach the point where Grand Canary Island was in sight. Then the winds died, and the fleet was forced to sit in a quiet sea for two or three days. When the winds picked up again, the three ships made land. *Pinta* needed some repairs, so Columbus decided to have that done in the Canaries. Meanwhile, he went ashore and fell in love.

Doña Beatriz de Bobadilla was a beautiful young woman, still under thirty years old, whose husband had died. Columbus probably wished he had met her at another time. He wanted to be with her, but nothing was going to keep him from his voyage. Less than a week later, on September 6, 1492, the fleet weighed anchor again, fully repaired and loaded with additional food and fresh water.

Columbus now ordered the fleet to sail due west. Once the ships passed the island of Ferro, the men aboard were in uncharted seas. They expected that the next land they would see would be Antilia. But they did not know how far away it was. They forgot their dreams of wealth and adventure as they wondered what lay ahead of them.

Keeping a straight westward course was difficult at sea, where there were no landmarks as guides. Columbus and his pilots had compasses. These were round cards marked out with the four main directions, N, S, E, W, and with twenty-eight directions in between, like north by east, north, northeast, etc. North was marked by a lodestone, a piece of magnetized iron ore. Ships' compasses were enclosed in cases called binnacles, which protected them from the weather and also allowed them to swing freely with the motion of the ship. To sail west, they had to go at right angles to the direction of north.

Navigational instruments to figure out latitude depended on the stars. Based on the height of the North Star above the horizon, and where it was located in relationship to the two outer stars of the Little Dipper, sailors could get a rough estimate of latitude. They used an instrument called an astrolabe to compare the distances between these stars.

Time was measured by the half-hourglass. When the boy turned it, he would sing. There was a verse for each turn. Samuel Eliot Morison, who studied the life of Columbus for most of his own life, gave an example of the verse that was sung at "five bells":

> *Five is past and six floweth,*
> *More shall flow if God willeth,*
> *Count and pass make voyage fast.*

This helped give the sailors a sense of the passage of time. It was also a safety measure. Sometimes, a boy who watched over the sands of time would

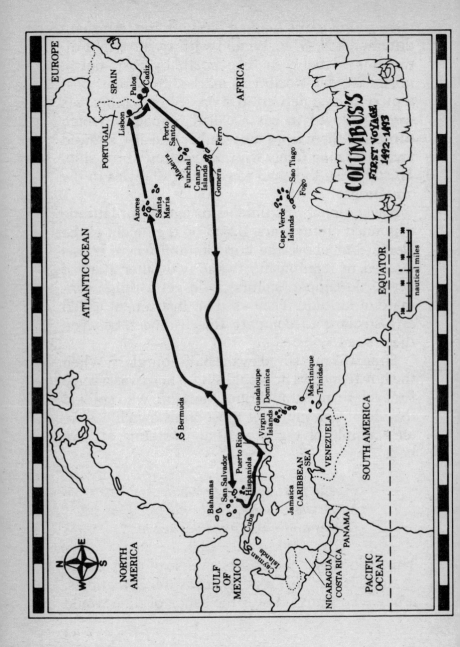

fall asleep or otherwise not do his timekeeping duty. If he didn't sing out when he should, someone was bound to notice.

The fleet enjoyed excellent weather for the first ten days or so. The sun shone, the sea was smooth, the winds carried the ships along at a fine clip. Birds that follow ships were in great abundance, giving the men something to watch and talk about. To them, the presence of birds also meant that land was not all that far away, even though no one could see it.

But along with the familiar sight of birds, there were unfamiliar and strange sights out in the vast Ocean Sea. One night the sailors were frightened when they saw a meteor fall. Columbus called it "a marvelous branch of fire." A day or so later, the three ships entered what came to be called the Sargasso Sea.

It is a sea within a sea, and its currents move so slowly that it is covered with huge amounts of floating seaweed. Columbus had heard about this sea, but it must have been fascinating for him to see the surface covered for miles with green and yellow weeds.

By the eleventh day out, everyone started searching the horizon more closely for land. By Columbus's calculation, the ships were supposed to be near the Isle of Antilia. The presence of birds seemed to support Columbus's calculations. But the sailors had no way of knowing that some kinds of birds, like storm petrels, can live far out at sea for months at a time. Then the winds changed, slowing the ships, and the sea calmed so they made little headway. It was frustrating not to be able to move at a good speed, and when someone on the *Pinta* shouted that he had sighted land, all were relieved.

Everyone, including Columbus, thought he saw an island on the horizon. The captain general gave thanks to God and ordered all hands to sing a hymn to the Almighty. By dawn the next morning, however, the sailors were forced to admit that what they had seen had been a cloud bank on the horizon. They had not found the Isle of Antilia, or any other island, for that matter.

By the first of October, the sailors were beginning to feel the monotony of life at sea. As far as they could see, north, east, south, or west, there was nothing but a vast ocean that met an even vaster sky. Mealtimes broke up the day, but the food was basically the same — biscuits and salt pork, with fresh meat only occasionally. It was difficult to get a good night's sleep on shipboard, especially for the common seamen. While captains and navigators had bunks, the seamen simply went to sleep on the wooden planks on the decks or below decks.

By that time, the men on the three ships had already set a record. At least in recorded history that we know about, they were the first to have been at sea more than three weeks without sighting land. Tired and grouchy, the men had begun to fight among themselves over petty differences. The officers of the three ships had to allow the men to fight enough to get the anger out of their systems, but not enough to really hurt one another. The men had also begun to grumble, to talk about how this was a voyage to nowhere, that their captain general didn't know where he was going. Such a mood among sailors had many times before led to mutinies, and everyone on the three ships knew that.

Luckily, within a few days there began to be signs of land — debris floating in the water, a ridge of clouds, birds that were known to be land birds. In fact, the sailors began to see flocks of birds. And Columbus changed the course of his ships from west to southwest to follow them. The men stopped grumbling, and each concentrated on being the first one to sight land.

On Thursday, October 11, Columbus noted in his journal that men on the *Pinta* had found a piece of wood floating in the water. It had been carved, probably with iron. That had to mean they were near land.

At ten o'clock that night, Christopher Columbus himself was standing on the high bridge of the *Santa María* when he saw a strange light. He did not know what it was, and neither has anyone since. It may have been worms that are called palolo worms and are native to the West Indies and Bermuda. They come to the surface to spawn a couple of nights after the full moon. Their hind parts glow, and they cast an eerie light.

The light may also have been moonlight reflecting off a land mass. Whatever it was, it was a great sign of hope to Columbus and his men, and about four hours later one of those men sighted land.

Which island it was has long been the subject of argument among historians and navigators. More than one modern seaman has tried to retrace the voyage of Columbus, using the paraphrases of his journals. But they could not be sure of his distances, and especially of his speed, since he had no way of accurately measuring it. In the 1980s, the National Geographic Society hired a professor at the University of Florida named Eugene Lyon to do a new translation from Spanish into English of the documents about Columbus's first voyage. Then a team from the National Geographic Society put all the information they had into a computer. This included knowledge of ocean currents and winds, as well as Columbus's own information. The computer concluded that Columbus's first landfall had to have been at what is now known as Samana Key in the Bahamas. A voyage to that island, which is now uninhabited, sponsored by the National Geographic Society, showed that it is just as Columbus described. An archaeological dig on the island, carried out by the Florida State Museum at the University of Florida, found pieces of broken pots and other signs that people lived on the island in the time of Columbus. Modern science and computers can be very helpful in finding out the truth about history.

On the morning of Friday, October 12, the three ships anchored. Columbus went ashore in a small armed boat. People gathered at the beach to meet the party. All were naked, and all were under thirty years old. They were a handsome and sturdy people, with the widest brows and heads Columbus had ever seen. The reason was that it was the custom of those people, the Lucayan, to bind the heads of babies so that they would grow wide. Wide heads were, for them, a sign of beauty.

The Lucayan were decorated with black, white, and red paint. They traveled in boats "made of the trunk of a tree," some of them large enough to hold forty men. They called these boats *canoa*, from which our word *canoe* comes. Columbus noticed that many of the men had scars on their bodies. Using sign language these men explained that people came from nearby islands and tried to capture them.

Columbus wasted no time ordering his men to plant the Spanish flag on the island, claiming it for the Spanish Crown. He named the island San Salvador, for Jesus Christ ("Holy Savior"). That done, he ordered the refilling of the water casks, for what water they had left had acquired a life of its own in the tropical climate and was hardly fit to drink. Then, he and his men started trading with the Lucayan. In exchange for the red caps, glass beads, and little bells Columbus had brought, the Lucayan offered parrots, cotton thread, and spears tipped with fish teeth. Based on Columbus's notes, the Lucayan would have been just as happy to give these things to the strangers. He described them as very generous and loving.

Using sign language (the Lucayan did not understand Arabic, so Columbus's translator was of no use), the natives told Columbus that there was a land to the west and also to the northwest, from which men often came to battle with them. There was also land to the south, where a king with much gold lived. Columbus decided to find that king.

In the meantime, while his ships underwent needed repairs and his crew got a chance to feel land under their feet, he and a few men set out in a rowboat to explore around the island. After a few hours, he returned, and the three ships weighed anchor and set out to explore the nearby islands. They took with them six Lucayan to act as guides, although the Lucayan would have preferred to stay where they were and were taken against their will.

Columbus named the next island Santa María de la Concepción after the Virgin Mary. Today, it is known as Crooked Island. There he found people who were equally pleased with the goods he had for trade, but who also had no gold except for a few ornaments that they said they had gotten elsewhere. No amount of sign language could help Columbus find out just where that was.

Columbus was fascinated by the wildlife he saw on and around the islands. In the waters were whales and brightly colored fish that quickly lost their colors when they died. In the shallows around Crooked Island he saw a *serpent, which we killed. . . . When it saw us, it threw itself into the lake and we followed it in, because it was not very deep, until with lances we killed it.* He described it as about six feet in length.

It was probably a crocodile. William Keegan, an assistant curator at the Florida Museum of Natural History at the University of Florida in Gainesville, used descriptions based on Columbus's journals to try to identify the site of the village where Columbus spotted the "serpent." During an excavation of the site, a crocodile bone and tooth were discovered. The site dates to around 1492, but no one can be sure if the bone and tooth belong to the crocodile Columbus killed.

The third island was named Fernandina after King Ferdinand. It was a huge island, also inhabited. Columbus notes that the local people here were a bit different from the Lucayan on the other two islands: *a somewhat more tractable and domesticated people . . . they know better how to bargain. . . . I know of no sect whatever, and believe they would very shortly become Christians, because they are of very good intelligence.*

Since Columbus had at first described the Lucayan as generous and loving, he may have changed his opinion of them based on his experience with the six he had forced to accompany him.

Columbus didn't remain on the island long enough to discover the inland limestone caves where carved ceremonial stools and religious figurines were used in worship. However, he did stay long enough to marvel at the trees he found, and he reported that in one case several different kinds of branches grew on one trunk.

But Columbus was looking for gold, and he set out for the fourth island, which he named Isabella, after the queen of Spain. Today it is called Fortune Island, which would have been fitting during Columbus's visit, too, for it was here that his Lucayan guides told him the king with the gold lived. The fleet waited off the island for several days, hoping the king would appear. When he did not, Columbus did not launch an expedition to find him.

The reason was his Lucayan guides. He was afraid that if he anchored, they might escape and make it home to San Salvador, which was only eight leagues (about twenty-eight statute miles) away. Meanwhile, one good thing about the fact that the Spaniards and the Lucayan had come to understand each other better was that he realized they were talking about a land that they called Colba. Columbus was certain that this land, which he called Cuba, must be part of either Japan or China. He headed there next.

While the small Bahama islands he had found yielded no gold, they added much to the knowledge and comfort of Columbus and his crew. They found maize, or corn; yams, or sweet potatoes; pumpkins; and a tree that Columbus guessed correctly would make good dye wood. The most important discovery for the crew was the hammock, which the Lucayan called *hamaca*. It was the natives' basic bed, made of woven cotton and slung between two trees. Before long, hammocks were being used aboard ships, drier and far more comfortable beds than the hard boards of a ship's decks.

Columbus's small fleet reached Cuba on October 28, 1492, anchoring off the north shore. Since he never sailed around the island, he had no way of knowing at that time that it was an island. He thought it was part of the mainland of Asia. India was not far away, he decided, and so he called the people he met Indians.

The "Indians" were friendly and eager to please. Questioned about gold, they spoke about a place whose name sounded like Cubanacan, by which they meant mid-Cuba. But Columbus was so set on the idea that he had reached China that he decided they were saying something like "El Gran Can." This could only be the fabled Chinese emperor, the Grand Khan, about whom Marco Polo had written.

Columbus immediately sent a party to establish diplomatic relations with the emperor. Luis de Torres, who could speak Arabic, was in charge. Also along was a seaman named Rodrigo de Xeres, who had once met an African king in Guinea and so knew how to act around royalty. Accompanied by Indians who carried Columbus's official letter of introduction to the Chinese emperor and various gifts, the two Spaniards trekked into the interior. They expected to find a great imperial city. Instead, they found a large village of thatched huts and friendly people with no gold.

While the official party was away, Columbus set

about finding proof that he had indeed reached China. He collected samples of plants that seemed to be like those he had heard and read about. There was a shrub that smelled something like cinnamon, and he took a specimen of that. There were some roots that the fleet's surgeon thought were Chinese rhubarb, a drug valued in Europe. There was creole pepper that seemed like it might be the kind of pepper obtained in China.

When the official party returned with the bad news that they had been unable to find the Grand Khan, they did have interesting stories to tell. One of the most intriguing was of the rolled-up leaves that the natives of Cuba lit with a firebrand, inhaling the smoke. They called the cigarlike rolls *tobacos*.

The Indians kept saying that there was gold in Cuba, and the fleet spent several weeks putting in at different harbors in pursuit of this treasure. At one point, the captain of the *Pinta*, Martín Alonso Pinzón, took off with his own ship in the hope of being the first to find gold. (He was not successful.) He would not be in contact with Columbus again until the return home. Columbus was furious with Pinzón for this disobedience, but there was not much he could do in a strange land thousands of miles from home. Time was running out. Soon, he would have to return to Spain, and he still had not found any gold.

After a while, the Indians started talking about another land where gold could be found. By this time Columbus was getting desperate. No other proof that he had found the Indies would suffice if he could not find gold. Early in December the *Niña* and the *Santa María* set out to cross the Windward Passage, arriving off the coast of Haiti on December 6. It was the day when the sailor saint, and the favorite saint of children, St. Nicholas, was traditionally honored, and so Columbus called the harbor San Nicolas Mole. He called the land La Isla Española, "Island of Spain," because its beauty reminded him of Spain. Today, we call it Hispaniola.

On this island of Hispaniola Columbus at last found gold. The Taino Arawak people who lived there were all wearing gold jewelry. Eventually, Columbus received an invitation from Guacanagari, a *cacique*, or ruler, in the northwestern part of the island, and the two ships set off for Caracol Bay. Reaching the harbor, and calm waters, on Christmas Eve, the admiral decided to get his first sleep in forty-eight hours. So did the helmsman of the *Santa María*, who handed over the tiller to a small boy. Around midnight, the ship settled onto a coral reef. The boy sang out in alarm, but by the time Columbus and the captain arrived, the damage had been done. The ship had run aground, coral heads were tearing holes in her bottom, and the hull was filling up with water. Columbus gave the order to abandon ship.

With the help of daylight, and of men sent by Guacanagari, the seamen tried to free the ship from the reef. But they were unsuccessful. All they could do was save the cargo, including the trading goods. Some of the Indians guarded the red caps, beads, bells, and other items, and Columbus later noted that not one thing was taken.

Christopher Columbus firmly believed that God was with him on the journey, and so he decided that the *Santa María*'s accident was a sign. He was meant to establish a colony there. So, he ordered his men to build a fortified camp with timbers salvaged from the grounded ship. Guacanagari was pleased with the idea, for he believed it would help him against his enemies on other parts of the island. Columbus named the camp Villa de la Navidad (Christmas Town). He had no trouble getting volunteers to man the camp. Most of the crew from the *Santa María* volunteered, as did some from the *Niña*. Altogether, there were thirty-nine volunteers, including a carpenter, a caulker, a doctor, a gunner, a tailor, and a cooper. Everywhere they looked they saw evidence of gold, and they had plans to trade for as much of it as they could. To aid them, Columbus gave them most of the trading goods he had left, plus as many provisions as he could spare. He also promised to return as soon as he could.

At this point, however, it was time to set sail for Spain. He had accomplished what he had set out to do, or at least he thought he had. He believed he had found the Indies, had established a colony, and had enough proof of his discovery to take back to Ferdinand and Isabella. He began making plans to return to Spain on the *Niña*, hopefully along with the *Pinta*, if he could find her. At sunrise on January 4, 1493, with still no sign of the *Pinta*, Columbus set sail for home.

5
Admiral of the Ocean Sea

For three days the *Niña* sailed east along the coast of Hispaniola. Then, suddenly, another ship was sighted. It was the long-lost *Pinta*. Angry as he was with Pinzón for going off on his own, Columbus was relieved that he would now have two ships making the return crossing of the Ocean Sea.

Pinzón went aboard the *Niña* to report to Columbus. He had not found gold where he had expected to, but he had found it elsewhere. He'd been about to investigate when he'd learned from the Indians of the wreck of the *Santa María*. He had turned back to help Columbus. Columbus believed the explanation and decided to investigate the place where Pinzón had found gold when he made his next voyage to Hispaniola.

While waiting for favorable winds, Columbus did more exploring of the Hispaniola coast. Men sent ashore for fresh water discovered large gold nuggets at the mouth of a river, which Columbus named the River of Gold. A few days later, they encountered the first armed Indians they had met, but they managed to avoid serious trouble. They even persuaded a couple of them to join the group of Lucayan whom they were taking back with them to Spain.

At last, on January 16, the two ships headed north, where they hoped to catch strong westerly winds that would enable them to head east. They crossed the Sargasso Sea under a full moon, and all aboard must have taken heart at the sight of the meadow of weeds that they had crossed on their voyage out. On the last day of January, the ships turned east, and aided by the strong winds made excellent speed for several days.

Within a week, however, the winds had turned blustery and the ocean stormy. The small ships fought to survive in the turbulent sea. On the night of February 13, the two ships lost sight of one another in a storm, a frightening thing for everyone. By the following morning, everyone on the *Niña* was praying to St. Valentine and to the Virgin Mary. Columbus was afraid that all would perish and the rest of the world would never know about his exciting discoveries. In desperation, he wrote out the basic facts of his route and his discoveries on a piece of parchment, wrapped it in waxed cloth, and then placed it in a barrel, which he threw overboard. This barrel has never been found.

The following day, to the relief of everyone on the *Niña*, land was sighted. They had reached the Azores. They put in at Santa María, and everyone flocked to a little church that was dedicated to the Virgin. While they were praying, they were seized by a group of village men and put in jail. The Portuguese captain of the island thought they had just returned from an illegal trip to West Africa (only the Portuguese king could order such voyages). Fortunately Columbus was able to straighten out the matter and get his men back.

At sea again, the *Niña* encountered more storms and then a hurricane. Her sails were in tatters by now, but there was nothing to do but to try to continue under bare masts. Columbus and his crew were pretty tattered themselves, for they were exhausted from fighting the storms, and reduced to eating scraps because food supplies were so low. Describing himself in his journal, Columbus wrote: *very crippled in my legs, owing to having been constantly exposed to the cold and water, and owing to the small amount I have eaten.*

Off course and headed straight for Portugal, Columbus decided not to try to make it to Spain. Instead, he would put in at the Tangus River and dock at Lisbon. He knew he was taking a risk, for he was sailing under the flag of Portugal's maritime rival, Spain, but he saw no other way.

Also moored at Lisbon when the *Niña* arrived was the large warship commanded by Bartholomew Diaz, the Portuguese explorer who had first rounded the Cape of Good Hope at the tip of

Africa. Diaz was very helpful and offered to aid Columbus in getting his ship refitted and re-provisioned.

King John of Portugal summoned Columbus, and Columbus worried about visiting the Portuguese king before the Spanish queen who had supported him. But he knew he had to accept. He took with him some of the healthier Indians as proof that he had been nowhere near Africa. The Indians proved to be of great help to Columbus. In addition to being obviously a different people from Africans, they were able to tell the king all about the area from which they came. With beans, they created a map of what would later be called the Lesser Antilles, a group of islands south of the island chain that Columbus had found. Columbus was free to return to Spain.

Meanwhile, the *Pinta*, captained by Martín Alonso Pinzón, had made a slightly easier crossing and had made port in northern Spain at the end of February. Pinzón had sent word to the king and queen in Barcelona, hoping that he would be able to give them the news of the exciting discoveries to the west. But the royal couple sent back word that they would wait to hear the news from Christopher Columbus. Embarrassed, Pinzón set out for his home port of Palos.

The *Niña* and *Pinta* arrived at Palos on the same tide, the *Niña* arriving just ahead of her long-lost sister ship. When he saw the *Niña* already there, Pinzón could take no more. He went directly to his home near Palos and died within a month. The long voyage, and his failure to win what he thought was the acclaim he was due, proved to be too much for Pinzón.

For his part, after resting and eating properly for a few days, Columbus finished his journal. Here are the final words he wrote:

> *Of this voyage I observe that the will of God hath miraculously been set forth (as may be seen from this journal) by the many signal miracles that He hath shown on the voyage and for myself, who for so great a time was in the court of Your Highnesses, with the opposition and against the opinion of so many high personages of your household, who were all against me, alleging this undertaking to be folly, which I hope in Our Lord will be to the greater glory of Christianity, which to some slight extent has already occurred.*

In other words, Columbus was saying "I told you so." He was bitter over the many years it had taken him to find support for the voyage, and he would never forgive those who had doubted him.

While still in Lisbon, Christopher Columbus had sent his official report of the voyage to the king and queen. Fearing that King John of Portugal might intercept it, once he got to Spain he sent a copy of the report by official courier. He also sent a copy to Cordova, where Beatriz was with his sons, Diego and Ferdinand. He wanted to make certain that at least one copy of that report would not go astray.

Around the end of the first week in April, he received a letter from Ferdinand and Isabella. It was addressed to "their Admiral of the Ocean Sea, Viceroy and Governor of the Islands he hath discovered in the Indies." It commanded him to visit them at court. Columbus was overjoyed. All the titles he had asked for had been granted to him. He was famous and honored. And as soon as he could get back to the Indies he would also start getting rich.

He immediately wrote a report to the king and queen explaining how he intended to go about colonizing the islands. Two thousand settlers would be taken to the islands. They would include only Spaniards. No foreigners, Jews, people who spoke against the Church, or people who did not believe in God would be allowed. The settlers would set up towns in return for a license to trade with the islanders for gold. The settlers would have to go into the interior of the island to find natives who were willing to trade for gold, but at specified times of year they must return to their towns and hand over their gold for smelting. The fifth part, or twenty percent, for the king and queen would be deducted at that time, as well as a tax for the Church. At certain times of year, there would be a ban on gold trading so that the settlers would be sure to grow crops. The Indians could be easily converted to Christianity and made to work for the settlers as slaves. There might even be a profit to be made in exporting slaves to Europe.

Around the same time he sent this report to the king and queen, Columbus also wrote to his brother, Bartholomew, in France, telling him about the success of the voyage and inviting him to accompany him on the next one.

Columbus made careful preparations for his trip to the court of Ferdinand and Isabella. He bought a fine new suit of clothes. He invited some of his officers to accompany him and made arrangements for six of the Indians to go along with him also. He ordered that they wear their best as well (feathers and fishbone and gold ornaments) and that they carry cages of parrots. It would be quite a procession.

The group set out for their visit to court, attracting crowds along the way. No one had ever seen anything like it. The Indians and parrots were the main attractions, but people also turned out to see the man who had crossed the Ocean Sea and found the Indies. Christopher Columbus must have loved the attention.

The group crossed Andalusia and entered Cordova to great fanfare. There, Columbus was reunited with Beatriz; his son, Diego, who was now thirteen years old; and five-year-old Ferdinand. They all joined the procession, and after a big celebration in Cordova continued on to Barcelona.

As the procession reached Barcelona, it seemed as if the whole city had turned out to welcome Columbus and his party. Crowds escorted him to the royal court. When he entered the hall and bowed to Ferdinand and Isabella, the two monarchs rose to greet him. After he knelt to kiss their hands, they did him the honor of asking him to sit in a chair to the queen's right.

From his place of honor, Columbus summoned the Indians with their parrots, and various servants to show the spices and gold that he had brought back. He told the king and queen about his adventures and about the riches of the lands he had found. Later, everyone went to a nearby chapel to give thanks to the Lord for Columbus's good fortune. Some people noticed that tears were streaming down the admiral's face.

Not long afterward, the six Indians were baptized in the Roman Catholic Church. How they felt about this event is not known. But Columbus was delighted and looked forward to converting all the native people on the islands he had discovered and intended to colonize. He did not plan to wait long to return to the Indies.

Ferdinand and Isabella supported his wish to return soon. After all, they wanted to establish the Spanish claim to the area with a real colony, not just a fortified village. By the end of May they had issued official instructions to Columbus. He was to set up a trading colony and to convert the natives to Christianity. He was also to do further exploration so as to be sure that Cuba was really the mainland of Asia, and a gateway to China and other eastern countries.

It took very little time to outfit the second expedition, which was to be far larger and better equipped than the first. In fact, it was the biggest overseas colonizing expedition that had ever been sent out by a European country up to that time. There were at least seventeen ships, loaded with enough supplies for a six-month voyage plus a period of colonization. This time, in addition to the sheep, goats, hens, geese, ducks, and hogs that were usually carried for fresh food on a voyage, there were horses and cattle. Columbus hoped that these animals would adapt to the climate of the Indies and multiply so they could be used for food and work.

The *Niña* was among the seventeen ships. The lead ship, by coincidence, was named the *Santa María*, like the flagship on the first voyage. At least 1,200 sailors, soldiers, and colonists would travel on these ships, as well as surgeons and craftsmen and six priests, whose job would be to convert the Indians. Five of the baptized Indians would return to their homeland with the fleet. The sixth stayed behind at the court of Ferdinand and Isabella.

In September, 1493, Christopher Columbus said good-bye again to Beatriz and his sons and made preparations for his second voyage to the Indies. Until the last, he looked for his brother, Bartholomew, whom he hoped would be able to go on the second voyage. But Bartholomew never came, and Columbus had to leave without him.

6
The Second Voyage

No journal written by Columbus of his second voyage to the Indies has survived, although there are accounts written by three men who were on the voyage, including Juan de la Cosa, who served as mapmaker. We know that Christopher's youngest brother, Diego, went along on that voyage. We know that the fleet set sail on September 25, 1493, out of the Spanish port of Cadiz. We also know that Columbus made first for the Canary Islands, as he had before.

After that, however, he took a different route, hoping to shorten the journey and to make new discoveries in the Lesser Antilles on the way to Villa de la Navidad. Based on information provided by the Lucayan, this time he sailed west by south. The fleet enjoyed excellent weather. Except for one storm at the end of October, they sailed briskly before the trade winds, the faster ships racing ahead until sundown each day, when the entire fleet regrouped around the lead ship, *Santa María*, so the admiral could give them instructions for the following day. As darkness fell, the ships' lanterns bobbed up and down with the gentle lap of the waves, giving all aboard a sense of security that had been rarely felt on the first voyage.

Unlike the seamen on the first voyage, the sailors on this trip had signed up in droves, eager to share in the treasure that they knew awaited them. They knew where they were going, and because of the ease of crossing they did not become grouchy and grumbly as the first crew had. Due to the good weather, this time the fleet made landfall in twenty-one or twenty-two days.

It was a Sunday when land was first sighted, and Columbus named the new island Dominica, the name it still carries today. Just as he had planned, he had reached what we now call the Lesser Antilles. As the morning light increased, other islands could be seen, and Columbus named them Santa María Galante, after his lead ship, and Todos los Santos (All Saints), because it was just a couple of days past All Saints Day, November 1. The islands still carry these names.

After searching in vain for a harbor, Columbus finally ordered the fleet to anchor off Santa María Galante. He went ashore and planted the flag of Spain. He sent men to do some exploring, but they found nothing of great interest. So, the fleet

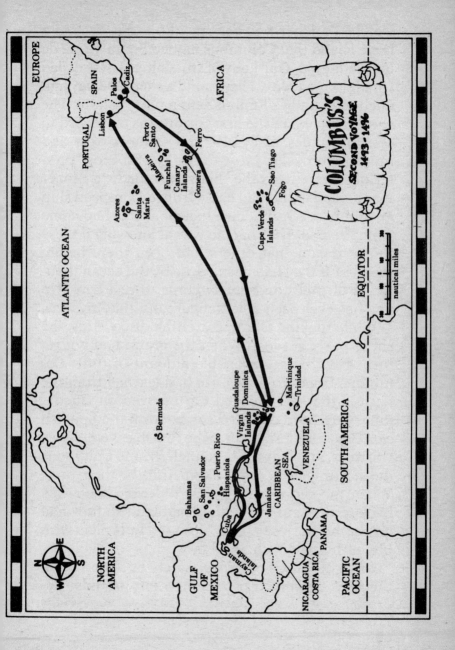

weighed anchor and continued on, this time to a large island that Columbus named Santa María de la Guadalupe (Our Lady of Guadalupe). It is called Guadaloupe today. They found a sheltered bay and anchored, and Columbus sent a party ashore. The shore party were the first Europeans on record to see pineapples. They also saw tame parrots and more hammocks. Most exciting, and most mysterious, were two other finds they made: a timber that looked as if it had come from a European ship and an iron pot that also looked as if it had come from Europe. They had no way of knowing if these things meant that others had been there before them, or if they had been borne by the ocean thousands of miles and finally come to rest here. No one has ever been able to figure out that mystery.

While making all these exciting discoveries, the shore party got lost. When the group had not returned within a reasonable amount of time, Columbus began to worry. He had learned from the natives that the dreaded Caribs lived on Guadalupe. Our word *cannibal* comes from the Spanish *canibale*, or flesh-eater. The Caribs were fierce warriors, and they ate human flesh, and Columbus did not intend to leave his men to be their prey. When the shore party finally did work their way back to the spot where they had landed, they had gruesome stories to tell of deserted huts filled with bits of human flesh and limbs.

Once the shore party was safely back on board, the fleet continued on, seeing more islands. Columbus named almost all of them after the Virgin Mary. He only stopped at one, which he named Santa Cruz, and which is now known by the French name, St. Croix. He later regretted choosing that particular island to land on.

He probably stopped there because it appeared to be inhabited. Instead of dense forests, he saw fields. At the head of a harbor, he saw a small village, and so he anchored in the harbor and sent a party of armed men to investigate. The villagers ran away when they saw the boat approaching. But when the boat started back for the flagship, it met up with a canoe of six Caribs, four men and two women, who were armed with bows and poison-tipped arrows. The Caribs attacked the Spaniards, wounding two, and put up a great fight before being captured and taken on board. It was the Spaniards' first experience with warrior women.

Columbus wasted no time getting away from Santa Cruz. He set off for other islands. As he approached the ones he had seen from Santa Cruz, he realized there were hundreds of small islands. Rather than name each one individually, he decided to call them Las Once Mil Virgines, after the legendary 11,000 virgins who had set out from Cornwall on the British coast on a pilgrimage to Rome and were later been killed by Huns at Cologne in Germany. These islands are still called the Virgin Islands.

The fleet continued its explorations, finally reaching the large island at the top of the chain, which we now call Puerto Rico. Columbus named it San Juan Bautista, after St. John the Baptist.

Columbus had yet to attend to the main purpose of his second voyage, which was to establish a colony. So, around the third week of November he ordered the fleet westward toward Hispaniola, the island where he had set up the town of La Navidad. On the way, they passed Cuba, and on a group of islands to the south of Cuba they discovered the green turtle. The natives fished for these large shelled sea dwellers using fish as bait, and the Spaniards found that the meat of the green turtle was very good to eat. Some experts say that Europeans could not have managed to explore the New World without the fresh meat of the green turtle. In later centuries, a tiny island in the middle of the South Atlantic called Ascension Island became a frequent stopping place for ships that crossed the Atlantic. Green turtles from Brazil 2,000 miles away bred there. The ships would load live turtles aboard, keeping the creatures on their backs to immobilize them. They would be kept alive for fresh food as the voyage continued. Ascension Island was such a common stop that a large rock with a hole in it near where the ships anchored was used as a mailbox by captains who left messages for other ships from which they had become separated at sea.

Reaching Hispaniola, Columbus decided not to go directly to La Navidad but first to anchor near a site that he thought might be a good place for a settlement. The shore party he sent to investigate returned with unsettling news. They had found the bodies of two men who had been dead a long time so they couldn't be recognized. But they had beards, and Indians did not have beards.

Columbus decided he had better go to La Navidad to find out how the rest of the men were faring. There, he learned that his first trading settlement had been completely wiped out. According to the natives, the Spaniards had roamed the island in gangs looking for gold and women. This had angered a chief named Caonabo, and he had ordered them all killed. Christopher Columbus had been wrong to think that all the natives were friendly.

The "lost colony of La Navidad" was forgotten for the next 500 years. But in 1986 a team of archaeologists from the Florida State Museum began to excavate there. They found bits of European pottery. They also found holes that may have been wells. Indians of the Caribbean have never dug wells, so if the holes were wells they were dug by people from Europe.

In one large hole the archaeologists found the jaw of a rat and the tooth of a pig. Both were European animals not known in that part of the world before Columbus.

Archaeologists may find more evidence of the lost colony, but it is doubtful that anyone will ever find out for sure what happened to the colonists.

One of the jobs of the men left behind at the Navidad settlement had been to scout out a proper site for a town. But if they had done so, they had left no record of their search. Now Columbus had to find a new site for his settlement. He ordered the fleet to sail eastward along the coast of Hispaniola in search of a good harbor. Sailing against the trade winds, the fleet was buffeted by high waves and continuous salt spray. When it at last dropped anchor on January 2, 1494, the spot was not ideal. But by that time a great number of livestock had died, and the crew and passengers needed fresh water. Several hundred men were sick, and food supplies were dwindling. Soon, there would not be enough left for the journey back home. Columbus was worried about the time he had wasted, with nothing to show for it but the discovery of more islands. He realized he must go ashore and get down to business. He decided to build his trading village where he landed and named it Isabella, after the queen of Spain.

While the colonists and some of the sailors set to work chopping down trees and digging a canal to bring water from the nearest river, Columbus organized an expedition to find the gold mine that was supposed to be in the interior of the island. This party found gold in the great central valley of Hispaniola and brought back a considerable amount, including three huge nuggets.

Columbus stared at these nuggets and worried that they weren't enough to send back to the king and queen after four months, but he decided they would have to do. He ordered twelve of the seventeen ships to return to Spain under the com-

mand of Captain Antonio de Torres. In addition
to an oral report about what had been accomplished that Torres was to give to the king and
queen (Columbus would furnish a full, written report when he himself returned), Columbus sent
the gold, sixty parrots, twenty-six Indians, spices
that he said were cinnamon and Malayan pepper,
and samples of what he called sandalwood.

Torres was to ask the royal couple to understand
that problems of illness and bad weather had delayed the expedition and to send as much food as
possible, as well as seeds and roots, clothing,
weapons, and livestock. He was to show the king
and queen the captured Caribs and mention again
the idea that Columbus had set forth in his report
after the first voyage: slavery. It might be a good
idea to hire men to raid the islands and capture
slaves for export. This would be another way to
make money, since the slave trade in other con-
quered lands had proved highly profitable.

Torres and his fleet of twelve ships set off for
Spain in early February and made the trip in just
twenty-five days. He immediately went to court to
present his goods and his report. Ferdinand and
Isabella agreed to send the food, seeds, arms, and
other things Columbus had requested. They told
Torres they could not make a decision about exporting slaves until they had more information.

While Torres was gone, Columbus placed his
brother, Diego, in charge of Isabella. Then he took
the remaining ships — he himself sailed on the
Niña — to do some more exploring of Cuba. By

this time, he had realized that Hispaniola was not Japan. Now he wanted to find out if Cuba was part of the continent of Asia.

The small fleet set out on April 24 and landed at Cuba about five days later. Columbus decided to sail south along Cuba's shore, for he believed the ancient theory of the Greek Aristotle that the farther south one sailed the more gold one would find. All along the way, they encountered friendly Indians, who fed them and traded with them. They also found more islands, like the one Columbus named Santa Gloria, which we now call Jamaica. Columbus continually marveled at the beauty of these islands, remarking about the scent of flowers and the singing of birds. He and his men saw their first flamingo on this expedition.

But Columbus looked in vain for any sign that they were in China. He saw no Chinese and no sights similar to those described by Marco Polo, like great stone palaces and Chinese "junks" (boats with bamboo sails). After weeks of sailing along the coast of Cuba, the ships were in need of repair and the men were grumbling. So, Columbus decided not to continue his exploration. Instead, he concluded that Cuba must be part of a continent because he had sailed along its coast far enough to be sure it wasn't an island. To support his decision, he had most of his men swear that they agreed with him. At this point, the men wanted to go home and were willing to swear to almost anything. But privately, many were not convinced.

The small fleet then set off for Isabella, making

little progress against the trade winds in deep waters. The admiral became ill as a result of lack of food and sleep and being continuously drenched by the spray of the sea. He may also have suffered a nervous breakdown, worried over all his responsibilities and especially over not having proved that he had reached China. When they reached Isabella at last, he had to be carried ashore by his men.

His brother, Bartholomew, was waiting for him at Isabella, and Columbus was overjoyed to see him. The two had not seen each other for six years. Bartholomew had never received the letter Christopher had sent him after the first voyage. He had learned of its success through the seamen's grapevine. He had set out for Spain, only to arrive after Columbus had set off on his second voyage. But he had visited Ferdinand and Isabella, and they had put him in charge of a fleet of ships that would take food and provisions to Isabella.

Unfortunately, once he had reached Isabella, Bartholomew's fleet had been stolen. A group of rebellious Spaniards, led by Fray Buil, the priest who was supposed to be in charge of converting the local people, had seized the three ships and headed back to Spain. That was only part of the troubles that awaited Columbus in Isabella. Things there had not gone at all as he had planned. Sailors and colonists had gotten into conflicts with the natives, had enslaved some of them, and stolen all the gold they could find. Christopher Columbus's younger brother, Diego, had been unable to control them. Part of his problem was that the Spanish colonists did not want to be ordered around by an Italian.

A few weeks later, Captain Antonio de Torres arrived at Isabella with four ships filled with supplies for the settlement. He also had a letter for Columbus from the king and queen. In it, they asked him to leave Isabella in the charge of one of his brothers and return to Spain to help them negotiate with the Portuguese over ownership of the newly discovered islands.

But Columbus did not go back to Spain. He may have been too ill to travel. Another reason may have been the hurricane that hit the island and sank all four of the recently arrived supply ships. Other ships were badly damaged, including the *Niña*, which had to be refitted. Columbus also may have decided it was best to get the settlement under control first. He realized that Fray Buil and the others who had returned to Spain in Bartholomew's fleet would be criticizing him in front of the royal couple and spreading the word that he and his brother could not govern the colony. He did not know that they also said the gold found at Hispaniola was not real gold, which was untrue.

What he did know was that his men had not collected enough gold. He wanted to return with lots of it, so as to silence his critics. If he could not send gold, he wanted to send back something else that was profitable.

Still convinced that a Hispaniola slave trade would bring great profits, he ordered his men to round up as many Indians as they could. They had little trouble, what with the weapons sent from Spain and the lack of weapons and fighting spirit of the Indians. By the end of February, 1495, when Torres was set to return to Spain with his four ships, some 1,500 slaves had been rounded up. Torres's ships could take only about 500 of them. Columbus offered the rest to the colonists and sailors. Once they had made their choices, he freed the remainder. Several escaped, including a *cacique* named Guatiguana. He managed to gnaw with his teeth through the ropes that bound him.

Once Torres had left, Columbus devoted his energies to getting more slaves. The only way the Indians could avoid slavery was to bring gold. Once they had handed over all their gold jewelry, they were forced to get gold by washing grains of the ore from the sandy bottoms of streams.

Meanwhile, Guatiguana, the *cacique* who had escaped enslavement, was bent on getting revenge. He tried to unite the Indians of Hispaniola. When he was unsuccessful, he formed an army to march on Isabella. Learning of Guatiguana's plan to attack, Columbus, Bartholomew, and their men attacked the army of Indians. With their superior weapons and their horses, they won the battle easily. But now Columbus decided to build forts on the islands, using slaves to do the work.

While all this was going on at Isabella, Torres had reached Spain, but some 200 of the 500 slaves had died at sea. Half of the rest were sick by the time they landed. Most of them died not long afterward. Spaniards didn't think much of slaves from Hispaniola.

By this time, Ferdinand and Isabella were having second thoughts about putting so much trust in Christopher Columbus. They wanted to investigate the charges against Columbus that had been made by Fray Buil and others. They sent Juan Aguado, a colonist who had returned to Spain with Torres, back to Isabella to find out what was really going on. He commanded a fleet of four provision ships and arrived at Isabella in October, 1495.

He found a shrunken settlement of only 630 Spaniards. Of the 1,200 original settlers, many had either died or returned to Spain. They had not bothered to grow crops because they had no real intention of staying. They had agreed to be colonists because of the promises of riches and gold. They were deeply unhappy, and they wasted no time in telling Aguado how they felt.

Columbus realized he had better get back to Spain to give his side of the story. He named Bartholomew as the commander of the colony in his absence and ordered him to abandon Isabella and build a new settlement on the south coast of Hispaniola. On March 10, 1496, he set sail for Spain in the *Niña*, accompanied by a single ship, the *India*, which had been built at Isabella with the timbers from two of the original seventeen ships that had been wrecked in hurricanes. Many of the colonists insisted on accompanying him. There were also thirty Indians. The ships were very overcrowded.

Sailing against strong headwinds, the two ships took nearly four weeks to reach Guadalupe. There, Columbus sent a party ashore to gather provisions. That party was attacked by a group of armed Carib women, but managed to beat them off, and captured one woman and her daughter. Columbus decided to take them back to Spain.

They made slow progress. Supplies ran low. There were too many people aboard. Water was rationed. Some people suggested eating the Indians, starting with the Caribs, who were cannibals anyway. Others suggested throwing all the slaves overboard, so at least they would not have to eat any of the precious food. Columbus was against both ideas.

Fortunately they reached the coast of Portugal after a voyage of six weeks, and there they were able to reprovision. They continued on to Cadiz, the Spanish port from which Columbus had begun his second voyage so triumphantly nearly three years earlier.

7
Columbus Discovers a New Continent

Christopher Columbus believed that what happened to him was God's will, and so he felt that his troubles meant that God was unhappy with him. He wasn't sure why, and he thought long and hard about what he might have done to make God displeased. It would never have occurred to him that enslaving the Indians was wrong, since slavery was widely practiced in Europe and Africa and even in the Indies. He believed that the natives of Hispaniola and the other islands were heathens because they were not Christians, and so he didn't think that his Christian God cared about them.

No, there must have been something else he had done to make God angry. Perhaps he had committed the sin of pride by being too boastful after his first successful trip. Whatever he had done, he decided that he should be humble as a sign to God that he was sorry for the sin or sins he had committed. He started wearing a simple brown cloak like monks wore, and this is how he dressed for the rest of his life. He turned down invitations to stay in the homes of the wealthy while he waited for the command to appear at the Spanish court. Instead, he sought shelter in religious houses. He went to church often and prayed many times a day.

Still, when the royal invitation did come, he decided to form another grand procession that would impress the king and queen. He ordered the Indians who had survived the journey to Spain to dress in feather headdresses and gold ornaments, and to carry cages of brightly colored parrots as before. Once again, crowds turned out to watch the procession pass by.

Ferdinand and Isabella were then at Valladolid. With them were Columbus's two sons, Ferdinand and Diego, who had been selected as pages to the queen. The ruling couple received Columbus in a friendly way and were pleased with the large gold nuggets he had brought for them. Under different circumstances, they might not have been so friendly. Fray Buil and others had spoken out against Columbus. They were clearly disappointed in his failure to set up a proper town and in the amount of gold he had sent back. They had decided that the Hispaniola slave trade was not worth the trouble, since the slaves kept dying.

But they were prepared to forgive Columbus if he would help them keep the Spanish claim to the lands he had found. At the time, they were afraid that Portugal might try to claim those lands.

King John II of Portugal had died by this time. But his interest in exploration and trade lived on. Before his death, he had decided that across the Ocean Sea there existed a completely undiscovered world. He had made his decision based on his readings of French and Spanish geographers and mathematicians. These men believed that there was an order to the world. Europe was balanced by Asia. Africa also had to be balanced by a fourth part of the world. There must be another continent somewhere to the west below the equator. They called this continent or fourth part of the world the Antipodes, which means located at the opposite part of the earth.

King John II of Portugal had hoped to send an expedition to find the Antipodes. His successor, Manuel the Fortunate, planned to do so. He ordered an expert mariner named Vasco da Gama to command an expedition across the ocean. When Ferdinand and Isabella heard of this planned voyage of exploration, they decided that they had to continue to support Christopher Columbus and the colony he was trying to establish. For his part, Columbus also believed that there was a continent south of the Antilles. He had heard the Indians speak of it. He wanted very much to discover that continent.

Unfortunately the royal couple was short of cash at the time, and it was almost two years before Columbus was able to put his next expedition to-

QVI RATE VELIVOLA OCCIDVOS PENETRAVIT A*IDOS
PRIMVS ET AMERICAM NOBILITAVIT HVMVM

CHRISTOPHORVS COLVMBVS LIGVR INDIARV PRIM'INVEI A*1492

ASTRORVM CONSVLT'ET IPSO NOBILIS AVSV
CHRISTOPHOR' TALI FRONTE COLVMB'ERAT

Christopher Columbus, as depicted in a sixteenth-century engraving.

Christopher Columbus appearing before Queen Isabella.

King Ferdinand and Queen Isabella bid farewell to Columbus as he departs on his first voyage in 1492.

A wood engraving of Columbus's fleet on the first voyage.

Christopher Columbus on board the *Santa María* in 1492.

On the first voyage, after over two months at sea and still no land in sight, Columbus's crew threatens to mutiny.

Columbus and his crew spot land, as depicted in "The First Sight of the New World," an 1892 lithograph.

Columbus, reaching the new continent, jumps from a barge onto land.

A sixteenth-century engraving of Columbus encountering natives at Hispaniola.

A native chief informing his tribe of Columbus's arrival, as portrayed in 1890.

An 1892 engraving of the wreck of the *Santa María* off the coast of Hispaniola. This occurred on Christmas Eve, 1492.

Columbus's triumphant return to Spain in 1493. The captives he brought with him walk behind.

A copper engraving of Columbus at the Spanish court presenting an account of his voyage to King Ferdinand and Queen Isabella.

An 1892 lithograph depicts Columbus in chains, after his arrest in 1500.

Columbus in prison in 1500, depicted in a copper engraving.

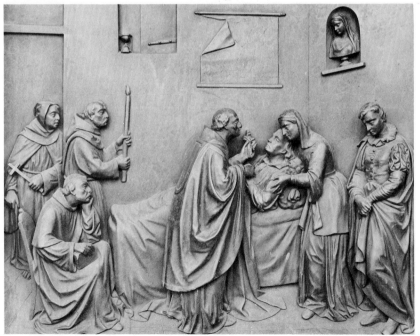

A panel on the huge bronze door at the Capitol in Washington portrays Columbus receiving the last rites before his death in Valladolid, Spain, on May 20, 1506.

gether. He had asked for five ships full of supplies, and three more ships for himself for exploring. He was given all eight ships that he requested. The supply ships were to be under the command of Alonso de Carvajal, who had commanded one of the ships on the second voyage. They were to sail directly for Hispaniola.

Of Columbus's three ships, one was the flagship, which he called *La Nao* (it means The Ship). The other two were the *Correo* and the *Vaquenos*. The faithful *Niña* was fitted out as a supply ship.

Recently an exciting discovery was made about the *Niña*. Dr. Eugene Lyon of the University of Florida found papers describing Columbus's favorite ship and the preparations for her third voyage under his command.

Dr. Lyon was in Seville, Spain, at the Archive of the Indies. He was looking through old documents to find out more information about Spanish shipping in the 1400s when he came across a bundle of papers called the *Libro de Armadas*, which means Book of the Fleets. In the bundle was a receipt written by a man named Pedro Frances for a ship he was to sail to Hispaniola in 1498. The name of the ship was *Niña*.

It was exciting for Dr. Lyon to discover that this was the same *Niña*, Columbus's favorite ship. The documents told about *Niña*'s history, including the two voyages with Columbus. They also told more. In 1497, *Niña* had been taken to Rome on a commercial voyage, without Columbus's permission. On the return trip to Spain, she had been hijacked off the coast of Sardinia by a French pirate. The pirate had stripped her of her artillery. The crew had managed to escape and return to Spain. Somehow, Columbus had managed to get her back.

The documents described in detail how *Niña* was fitted out and provisioned. She received new sails, a new 200-pound anchor, and new planking. Caulkers worked forty days on her deck and hull. She was fully armed with ten cannon and eighty lead balls, and 100 pounds of gunpowder. Individual weapons for the soldiers included fifty-four short and twenty long lances. These are the supplies that were loaded onto her: eighteen tons of wheat, seventeen tons of wine in pipe barrels, seven tons of sea biscuit, two tons of flour, over one ton of cheese, a ton of salt pork, and barrels of olive oil, garlic, sardines, and raisins.

The *Niña* and the *Santa Cruz*, another supply ship, also carried between them ninety colonists, including eighteen farmers, fifty crossbowmen, a priest, a locksmith, a miner, and a surgeon. The number of crossbowmen compared to farmers shows that Columbus realized he needed warriors more than farmers to tame the new land. The locksmith's job was to make sure no one who wasn't supposed to could get at either the supplies or the gold. He might also have been taken along to make locked places for holding slaves. The miner would have been taken along to teach the Indian slaves how to extract the gold from the earth. The priest was probably as much for the men aboard, who needed all the divine help they could get, as he was for converting Indians. And the surgeon was one of the most important men aboard, considering all the sickness that plagued the Europeans in the new lands.

The *Niña* and the *Santa Cruz* also carried four women. At least two of them were gypsies. They were named Catalina and Maria, and they were convicted murderers freed by the king and queen after they promised to go to Hispaniola. Many of the new colonists were criminals. By this time, most Spaniards would not go to Hispaniola unless it was a way to get out of jail. Columbus's reason for sending women to the colony was to start families, which he hoped would help make the settlement a more permanent one.

The two ships set sail for Hispaniola in January, 1498. Columbus's three ships, along with the three other supply ships, didn't leave until the last week of May. It was the same week that Vasco da Gama, sailing under the Portuguese flag, arrived in India.

The fleet stopped off at Grand Canary Island, where the fleet loaded up with cheese. From there, the three supply ships left for Hispaniola. Columbus would take a different, more southerly course. He planned to sail down to what he thought was the latitude of Sierra Leone in Africa. Gold had been found there. According to the theory of balance in the world, if he sailed west, he would find gold at the same latitude on the other side of the world. He made a stop at the Cape Verde Islands, where he had planned to take on livestock. But the heat was so intense that many of the crew members aboard got sick. Columbus also must have had trouble bargaining for the cattle, because he left without taking any on.

He got under way on July 7, placing his voyage this time under the protection of the Holy Trinity. Within a week, the winds had slowed to fitful breezes. The small fleet was in the doldrums, that part of the ocean near the equator where hardly a wind stirs.

Even now, sailors dread the doldrums, and being in them must have been frightening for Columbus and his seamen who had never experienced them before. They had never gone through a whole day when there wasn't at least some wind. Now there were days on end when there was nothing but a light breeze. The ships drifted closer and closer to the equator while the heat became more and more oppressive. No one could stand being below decks, for the heat was at its worst there. Yet, when they were on deck the sun beat down on them like fire. People fought over the tiny bits of shade. At night, no one moved from the deck, because at least there one had a chance of relief from the small breezes that stirred now and then.

For the cook, it was at least nice not to have to worry about his great copper pot, which hung over a fire in a sandbox on deck. There were no winds or high tides to tip it over. But it was too hot to eat. And the fresh water, loaded on at the last port, had become alive with tiny creatures that thrived in the heat and humidity. Tempers were short, and

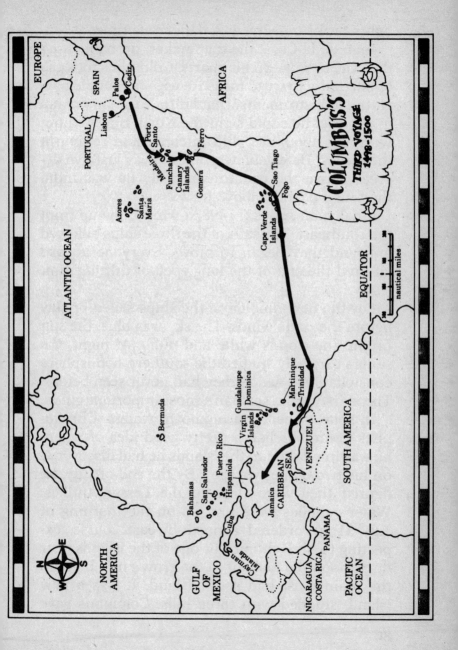

fights broke out. It was a dangerous time.

Juan de la Cosa, the mapmaker, probably used the time to work on his charts. Columbus took the opportunity to try to measure with his simple navigational instruments what latitude the ships were in. At least he could sight the North Star without worrying about the ship pitching and rolling in the waves. He calculated that he was just five degrees above the equator. Actually he was more than nine degrees above it.

Finally, on July 22, 1498, a wind came up from the southeast. The sails of the three ships billowed out, and they began to move. Everyone aboard cheered the end of the long spell of drifting aimlessly.

For the next nine days, the ships sailed briskly before the trade winds. The sky was blue, the sun bright, the clouds white and puffy. At night, the sailors excitedly studied the southern hemisphere constellations, which they had never seen before. The stars were a seaman's most important guide.

In spite of being in unknown waters, Christopher Columbus had a pretty good idea of where he was in relation to the islands he had discovered on his two earlier voyages. By the end of July, he figured they were close to the Lesser Antilles. Water supplies were low, so on the morning of July 31 he ordered a north-by-east course, expecting to hit Dominica or one of the islands near it. By noon the lookout in the crow's nest high up the main mast had spotted land. It was a new island, studded with three hills. Columbus gave thanks and named it Trinidad, after the Holy Trinity.

The ships sailed along the south coast of Trinidad looking for a bay with a river emptying into it so they could get fresh water. The one they found is now called Erin Bay. Just before turning into it, Columbus caught a glimpse of another land mass. He did not know it, but it was his first sight of South America.

After taking on fresh water and giving the sailors time for a swim, Columbus decided that he should find a more protected harbor. The ships sailed further along the coast of the island until they found one. Then Columbus gave the signal to drop anchor, and all aboard went ashore for a few days of badly needed rest.

While the others fished and swam, Columbus looked with hope for signs that would tell him he was near China. He was deeply disappointed when the natives turned out to be very similar to the Lucayan and Caribs.

When the ships weighed anchor a few days later, Columbus decided to explore the land he could see to the north. Suddenly a huge tidal wave bore down upon them. It snapped the anchor line of the *Vaquenos* and lifted her up to the sky, then dropped her into the deep trough left in its wake. This was a frightening experience. The great wave was probably caused by the eruption of a volcano on the mainland.

After recovering from the fright and repairing the anchor line, the small fleet continued its northward journey. They crossed what is known today as the Gulf of Paria and anchored off the Paria Peninsula, which Columbus thought was an island. They began to explore the coast, and on Sunday, August 5, anchored and went ashore near a village of thatched huts. This was the first time Christopher Columbus and his men set foot on South America.

Two days later, a group of natives appeared. They told the Spaniards that the place was called Paria. Columbus had stayed on board because his eyes were hurting, probably from scanning the horizon so often. He sent his senior captain, Pedro de Terreros, to plant the Spanish flag on this latest conquest for Spain. The natives were witnesses, but they had little idea of what the Spaniards were doing.

In exchange for the Spaniards' beads, sugar, and hawks' bells, the natives brought fresh fruit and a fermented drink like beer. They wore large polished discs made of a combination of copper and gold. They got the gold locally. They had to import the copper from Central America, and so of the two metals copper was more valuable to them. They gladly traded their gold and copper ornaments for the copper and brass pots the Spaniards offered them.

On another part of the coast, Columbus found women wearing necklaces of pearls. They were quite happy to trade them for beads and bells, but they didn't have a lot of extra pearls. Columbus asked them to get as many as they could for the next time he came. We do not know if they did. We do know that Columbus never returned.

Still convinced that he was exploring an island, Columbus kept looking for its end, or for an outlet to the sea. When he had not found one by August 11, he turned back to the east to the Gulf of Paria, and from there out into the Caribbean Sea. On the way out, a lookout spotted another island. It was the date of the Feast of the Assumption, so Columbus named it Asunción.

That night, writing in his journal, it suddenly dawned on Christopher Columbus that Paria was not an island at all. The river was so large that it was far more likely to belong to a continent than to an island. Also, they had found a freshwater sea, and that, too, was not likely to be found around an island. He remembered the Carib Indians talking about a mainland to the south of them, a place where there was much gold. And then there were the writers who had suggested the presence of another continent. A Roman Catholic scholar named Esdras, who translated the first two books of the Bible into English, wrote that there were seven parts to the world, one of water and six of dry land. All those bits and pieces of knowledge and theory came together in Columbus's mind that night. *I believe that this is a very great continent, until today unknown,* he wrote. . . . *And if this be a continent, it is a marvelous thing, and will be so among all the wise, since so great a river flows it makes a freshwater sea of forty-eight leagues.*

The following day another island was sighted. Columbus named this one Margarita, and it is still called that today. If he had spent some time exploring Margarita, he would have found all the pearls he could imagine. Ferdinand and Isabella would have been as pleased with them as with gold. But by now Columbus was worried about what was happening at his colony. He felt he could not explore any longer.

Columbus wrote more in his journal about the new continent, this time as if addressing the king and queen: *It would be the greatest thing for Spain to have a revenue from this undertaking; your Highnesses would leave nothing of greater memory. . . . And your Highnesses will gain these vast lands, which are an Other World, and where Christianity will have so much enjoyment, and our faith in time so great an increase.*

Columbus described the new lands as an *otro mundo* or other world. The more he thought about this, the more his imagination carried him away. Within a few days he was describing the new continent as the Garden of Eden. He based this idea on the fact that, in the Bible, the Garden of Eden is described as being in the East, and on the idea of many writers that it was the farthest point of the Far East.

He yearned to explore it more, but he had to reach Santo Domingo, the new town on Hispaniola. He charted a northwest-by-north course that he calculated would put him on the island of Saona off Hispaniola. He failed to take into account the strong westward equatorial currents, however, and wound up on the island of Alta Vela about 120 miles southwest of Santo Domingo. The fact that he had miscalculated bothered him a great deal, but at least he now knew more about the currents.

Columbus's ships were anchored off Beata Island on August 21 when they sighted a strange vessel. It turned out to be commanded by Bartholomew Columbus, who had moved the settlement from Isabella to Santo Domingo. Bartholomew was looking for the supply ships. That fleet, under the command of Carvajal, had managed to miss Santo Domingo. Colonists had seen the ships from shore, and Bartholomew had set out after them. Christopher and Bartholomew were delighted to see each other, and together they headed for Hispaniola.

8
Christopher Columbus in Chains

Santo Domingo — the present-day Ciudad Trujillo, the capital of the Dominican Republic — was a simple little town of thatched houses. But it already looked more permanent than Isabella had. It was located at the mouth of a wide river, so it wasn't necessary to dig a canal for water. But the settlers of Santo Domingo had experienced many of the same troubles as the inhabitants of Isabella.

Columbus learned that there had been another rebellion, this time led by Francisco Roldán, whom he had appointed chief justice of Hispaniola. Roldán, a Spaniard, resented being under the rule of Italians. He had joined forces with Guarionex, the *cacique* of Maguana, and other local people in an attempt to take over the colony. When Bartholomew led a force after them, Roldán and about seventy armed men retreated to the south-western part of the island, an area called Xaragua.

As luck would have it, Xaragua was the place where Carvajal and the three supply ships had landed. The captain managed to hold onto the ships and the supplies, but not to some of his passengers. A number of men jumped ship and joined the rebels, increasing Roldán's force. With that greater force, he managed to capture a fort called La Vega in the center of the island.

Columbus and his brothers did not have enough strong men to recapture the fort. Many of the colonists were ill from the long voyage or from diseases contracted in the mosquito-filled swamps. So, the admiral decided to try to negotiate with Roldán. It took almost a year before they came to terms. Roldán came out the winner. All charges against him and his followers were dropped. He regained the office of chief justice. He and his men were also promised free passage home with all the gold and slaves they could take with them. Those who wished to stay were promised land in Xaragua. The only thing Columbus got in return was peace.

The agreement with Roldán also called for changing the basic structure of the settlement. Instead of a trading post, Santo Domingo would be run according to a system that would give each colonist his own plot of land and all the natives who lived on it as slaves. Each would be allowed to keep any gold he found on that land, minus the percentage that belonged to the Crown and to Columbus. Everyone at Santo Domingo liked that system better, because it gave them more control over their own lives. They felt more settled. Even the *caciques* preferred the new system. No longer were they forced to pay a hated gold tribute. The colony became better established as a result. Eventually that system would be used by the Spanish in most of their colonies in America.

In the summer of 1498, Columbus sent two of his three ships back to Spain. He stayed behind with *Vaquenos*. The major mission of *La Nao* and the *Correo* was to deliver Columbus's report to the royal couple. The ships arrived in Spain in the fall of 1498. A sailor named Alonso de Ojeda, who had been on Columbus's second voyage, got hold of Columbus's journal and charts. He was excited to read about the pearls at Paria and asked Ferdinand and Isabella for a license to make a voyage of his own to search for pearls.

Juan de la Cosa, Columbus's mapmaker on the two previous voyages, accompanied Ojeda. Also on Ojeda's voyage was a young man from Florence, Italy, named Amerigo Vespucci, who was then living in Seville, Spain.

Ojeda left Spain in early 1499 and followed the westward route of Columbus's third voyage. He reached Paria and collected a large amount of pearls. He also discovered the islands of Aruba and Curaçao. He found a gulf that the natives called Maracaibo. There, the natives built their huts on posts, or stilts, and Ojeda was reminded of Venice, Italy, where houses are also built above water. He named Maracaibo "Venezuela," meaning Little Venice.

Ojeda was not alone in using Columbus's discoveries for his own gain. Other captains were making voyages to find pearls. They included Peralonso Niño, who had once been the pilot of the *Santa María*, and Vicente Yañez Pinzón, former captain of the *Niña*. Christopher Columbus was supposed to be lord of all the lands he had discovered. But by this time Ferdinand and Isabella were more interested in their percentage of the treasures brought back than they were in Columbus's rights. Besides, if they did not license these voyages, they knew that captains and pilots would go anyway. This way, they at least got a share of what was brought back.

The Spanish court was receiving more and more complaints about the rule of Columbus and his brothers at Hispaniola. Columbus's son, Ferdinand, who with his older half brother Diego was still a page at court, hated to hear about these complaints. He later wrote that Spaniards who had returned from Hispaniola would shout at the admiral's sons, "There go the sons of the Admiral of the Mosquitos, of him who discovered lands of vanity and delusion, the ruin and the grave of Castilian [Spanish] gentlemen!" It was clear that the Spaniards still deeply resented being governed by Italians.

Before they received Columbus's report that he had made peace with Roldán and started the new system of land grants at Hispaniola, the king and queen decided to send someone to the colony to see what was going on. They appointed Francisco de Bobadilla as a royal commissioner and gave him the power to do whatever was necessary to set things right. Bobadilla's departure was delayed for over a year. In the meantime, Columbus's report arrived at court, but it did not cause the sovereigns to change their minds about the need for Bobadilla's mission. Eventually he set out on his journey.

Bobadilla arrived at Santo Domingo on August 23, 1500, and was shocked to see the bodies of seven Spaniards hanging from the gallows. There had been yet another rebellion, which had been put down by the Columbus brothers with the help of Roldán. Only Diego Columbus was at Santo Domingo to explain to Bobadilla what had happened. The admiral was at La Vega, and Bartholomew was at Xaragua. Bobadilla didn't think much of the hanging of Spaniards, especially by Italians. It seemed to him that the rules of Spanish law had not been followed and that they had not been given a fair trial first. He decided that the colony was out of control.

The royal commissioner immediately took over the government. He placed Diego Columbus under arrest and had him put in the brig, or jail, of the ship on which Bobadilla had just arrived. He then sent a messenger to La Vega to command the admiral to return immediately. Meanwhile, he had all Christopher Columbus's possessions placed under lock and key. Thinking that he might need the colonists behind him, he declared a general freedom to gather gold anywhere, not just on the lands that had been assigned to them. Then, he started interviewing colonists about what had been going on in Hispaniola.

As soon as Christopher Columbus received the summons to return to Santo Domingo, he got ready to go. He knew very well that trouble was in store for him, but there was nothing he could do. He was loyal to the Crown. And if any thoughts of rebellion had occurred to him, he quickly put them aside. He didn't have enough men loyal to him to make a stand.

As soon as Columbus reached Santo Domingo, he was put in chains and placed in the town prison. Not long afterward, Bartholomew also came back and was put in chains. There is some evidence that Bartholomew considered leading a force to Santo Domingo to free his brothers, but that Columbus advised him against doing so.

Soon, Bobadilla had a thick pile of statements from Spanish colonists that were critical of the Columbus brothers and the way they had run the colony. He decided he had enough evidence to put them on trial. Such serious business was always conducted in the home country, and this was true of all European colonies. Christopher and Diego were placed in chains aboard the ship *La Gorda*. Christopher's son, Ferdinand, later wrote that the captain of *La Gorda* didn't like seeing the famous explorer in chains and wanted to knock them off. But, Ferdinand wrote, his father would not let that happen, saying that only the king and queen could do that. Bartholomew, also in chains, was returned to Spain on another ship.

Columbus was deeply depressed about his situation. He felt he had done all he could, and more, for the king and queen. He had discovered a great Other World and taken possession of it in their name. He had fought against great odds, including unfriendly local people and disease-filled swamps, to try to build a colony. He had put down two different rebellions that had threatened that colony. But he was being treated as if he had been an unnecessarily cruel governor.

La Gorda arrived at Cadiz at the end of October, 1500. Columbus, still in chains and accompanied by his jailer, went to stay at the monastery of Las Cuevas in Seville. People turned out to see him pass. He must have been a pitiful sight, in his coarse brown cloak and chains. Some people would have remembered his proud processions of earlier years. At the monastery, Columbus waited for the royal summons for him to appear at court. That summons did not arrive until six weeks later. Columbus was relieved when it came. For one thing, the summons ordered him released from his chains. Other men might have thrown them away, but not Christopher Columbus. He kept them for the rest of his life as a reminder of what he had gone through. Another reason he was glad to get the summons was that finally he would have a chance to tell his side of the story.

All three Columbus brothers were commanded

to appear at court at the same time. Columbus's sons, Diego and Ferdinand, were still at court, so all five were together in the same place. Unfortunately, it was not a happy occasion. Diego and Ferdinand were upset to see their father looking so old and tired and were fearful of what might happen to him. Christopher Columbus must have been sorry that his sons had to see him in that condition.

The king and queen listened to what Columbus had to say and seemed to believe him. They promised him that he would receive justice, and that his privileges would be restored. But they took a long time to act on what they had said. In the meantime, many adventurers like Ojeda and Pinzón were getting wealthy on the pearls and other riches of the Other World.

While he waited for some official word from court, Columbus gathered together all the letters he had received from Ferdinand and Isabella and listed all the promises they had made to him. He still felt that he had the right to control the entire Other World. But the king and queen felt differently. After all, they had granted him rights and privileges over a "world" that they thought was a few islands. Now that a whole new continent had been discovered, they were not about to give control of it to one man. Especially not to a man who'd had so much trouble governing a single island. And especially not to a man who was not Spanish.

At last, in September, 1501, the royal word came. Bobadilla would be recalled from Hispaniola. But Columbus was not to return as governor. Instead, another man, Don Nicolas de Ovando, would be Governor of the Islands and the Mainland of the Indies (the royal couple still thought the new continent was the Indies). The new governor set sail in February, 1502, with a fleet that Columbus could only have dreamed about when he was trying to colonize Hispaniola. Ovando commanded no fewer than thirty ships and 2,500 sailors, soldiers, and colonists.

Columbus did get permission to send a representative along with Ovando so he could reclaim the possessions of his that Bobadilla had taken. The king and queen also said he could keep his titles of admiral and viceroy, although these titles now meant little.

By this time, Christopher Columbus was in his early fifties, which was old by the standards of the day. He had severe arthritis and other ailments. But he was in no mood to retire. His greatest achievements had been in exploring the Other World, and he wanted to make another voyage. He asked Ferdinand and Isabella for four ships and provisions so he could make a fourth trip to the Indies. A month after Ovando sailed, the court granted Christopher Columbus permission to make his fourth voyage of discovery.

9
The High Voyage Begins

By the time he left on his fourth voyage to the Indies, Christopher Columbus was a much different man than he had been on his first voyage. He was older and sicker, to be sure. But he was more knowledgeable about the great Ocean Sea that he had traversed a total of six times previously. (No one in Europe knew, still, that there was another great ocean, the Pacific, to the west of the new lands that had been discovered. The Indian Ocean, which Marco Polo had written about, is considered a mere bay, and not another ocean, in spite of its name.)

Columbus was also more aware of the hard blows that life could deal. He didn't expect to return from this voyage to great honors and privileges and wealth. He strongly suspected that the king and queen had agreed to this voyage mostly to get rid of him. They were grateful to him for discovering the Indies, but they didn't think much of his ability to govern the new lands, or to bring wealth to the Spanish throne. They had turned the administration of the colony over to another man. In fact, they forbade Columbus to go to Santo Domingo on his fourth voyage, fearful that there might be trouble between him and Ovando. They had given licenses to other captains to search for pearls and other riches. They just didn't want Columbus around, presenting petitions about what he thought he should have had. What he wanted out of this voyage was the best that a sea explorer can hope for: fair winds, sunny skies, a vast stretch of blue ocean, and, at some point that he could calculate with some assurance, a new and beautiful land never before seen by another European, or some exciting discovery that would change the way other Europeans traveled to the new lands.

He wanted to find out how his earlier discoveries related to Asia. He was still convinced that he had found the coast of Asia. Marco Polo had written about a strait, or narrow water passage, across which he had sailed from China to the Indian Ocean. Christopher Columbus, still convinced that Cuba was China, wanted to find that strait.

Columbus took his younger son, thirteen-year-old Ferdinand, along on this trip. Father and son sailed together on the largest of the four ships, each of which was about the size of the *Niña*. She was called *La Capitana*, because she was the flagship. The other ships were *La Gallega*, the *Santiago de Palos* (nicknamed the *Bermuda* after her owner Francisco Bermudez), and the *Vizcaina*. Bartholomew Columbus was a passenger on the *Bermuda*. He had not wanted to accompany his brother, but Columbus had said he needed him. A passenger who had volunteered to go on the voyage was Diego Méndez. He was educated and had a comfortable income. He may have volunteered because he wanted adventure or gold or both. He would prove to be a very important person on that voyage. Two others on that voyage were the Porras brothers, Francisco and Diego. One was to captain a ship, the other was the official comptroller, or treasurer. They were not men whom Columbus had chosen. Instead, they were along on the voyage because the Treasurer of Castile wanted them to be. The Treasurer of Castile was in charge of paying all the sailors and soldiers when the voyage was over. Columbus had no choice but to go along with his wishes. Still another passenger was an Irish wolfhound. Columbus believed the huge dog would be useful in scaring off unfriendly Indians.

A large portion of the crews of all four vessels were very young men, twelve to eighteen years old. Some Columbus scholars say that the admiral chose such young men for a reason: They were stronger, obeyed orders better, and were less likely to be able to compare his decisions to those of other commanders since they didn't have a lot of experience.

The fleet sailed from Cadiz on May 11, 1502,

and as usual headed first for the Canary Islands. From the Canaries, Columbus set the same course, west by south, as he had on the second voyage. The fleet enjoyed good weather, because it landed on Martinique, south of Santo Domingo, three weeks later. After three days at Martinique, where everyone rested and the ships took on fresh water, the small fleet sailed around the Antilles chain before heading for Santo Domingo.

In spite of the fact that he had been forbidden to go to Santo Domingo, Columbus believed he had good reasons for doing so. For one, he wanted to send letters back to Spain, and he knew that Ovando would soon be sending most of the ships in his great fleet to the mother country. For another, Columbus was not happy with the *Bermuda*. The ship was all right for carrying cargo, but it was difficult to navigate. Columbus wanted to trade that ship for one that would be easier to handle as he moved in and out of the islands. Finally, he could sense from the behavior of the sea and clouds and winds that a hurricane was coming, and he wanted to be in a protected harbor. He also wanted to be at a place where there would be materials, tools, and men in case any of his ships was damaged.

When the ships entered the harbor, Columbus sent his chief captain, Pedro de Terreros, ashore with a note addressed to Governor Ovando. In it, Columbus advised the governor of the coming hurricane, asked for permission to stay in the port until the hurricane had passed, and told Ovando

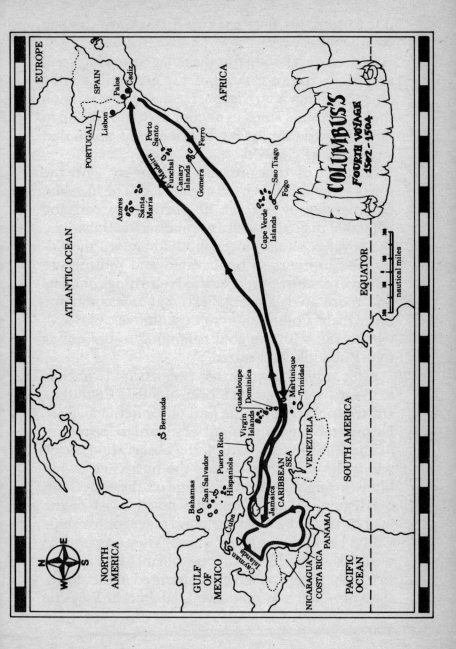

not to send his fleet back to Spain until the bad weather was over.

Ovando just laughed at the note. He read it aloud and made fun of Columbus for pretending to be able to predict a hurricane. He denied permission for Columbus's ships to anchor at Santo Domingo and directed that the big fleet leave for Spain that same day as planned.

Loading of treasure and passengers onto the thirty-ship fleet had been completed. The flagship, commanded by Antonio de Torres, was carrying $500,000 in gold as well as Francisco de Bobadilla, the royal commissioner who had caused the Columbus brothers to be arrested and returned to Spain in chains. Others carried returning colonists and more gold. The smallest, *Aguja*, was the one on which Columbus's representative, Carvajal, was to sail with the gold belonging to Columbus that Bobadilla had seized.

After receiving word that permission to anchor at Santo Domingo had been denied, Columbus started looking for a safe harbor for his small fleet. He ordered the ships to sail westward to the mouth of the Rio Jaina. Based on his observation of the winds, he had decided that the hurricane would blow through the Mona Passage off the eastern tip of Hispaniola and along the north coast of the island. Thus, the most sheltered place for his ships would be off the southern shore. They prepared as well as they could. Columbus told all four captains that if they were to become separated in the storm, the ships were to rendezvous at Puerto Viejo de

100

Azua, about fifty miles west. Then they waited.

By late afternoon, the winds had come up, and by dark the north wind was blowing at gale force. The anchor lines of the three smaller ships snapped, and the ships were forced out to sea. Fortunately their commanders managed to handle them so that none was lost. Captain Porras of the *Bermuda* became sick, and Bartholomew Columbus took over as captain, guiding the ship through the winds and waves.

It was a frightening experience. Having been through two earlier hurricanes in the Indies, Columbus respected the power of the hundred-mile-an-hour winds and the raging seas they whipped up. He worried especially about this hurricane because he had Ferdinand aboard, and Bartholomew on the *Bermuda*. He later wrote of the hurricane:

> *What man ever born . . . would not have died of despair when in such weather, seeking safety for son, brother, shipmates and myself, we were forbidden the land and the harbor that I, by God's will and sweating blood, won for Spain!*

Columbus's ships suffered some damage, but none sank or ran aground. The large fleet that Ovando had sent back to Spain against Columbus's warning was not so lucky. Nineteen of the ships sank with all on board. Six others also sank, but some of the passengers managed to survive. Four limped back to Santo Domingo suffering major damage. The only ship to survive the hurricane and make it to Spain was the *Aguja*, the one carrying Columbus's representative and his gold.

When the hurricane was over, Columbus's four ships met up with one another at Puerto Viejo de Azua as planned. They spent the next several days there, resting and making repairs. Then they sailed west, crossed the Windward Passage between Hispaniola and Cuba, then headed out across the Caribbean Sea. They landed on one of the Bay Islands off Honduras.

On that island, Bonacca, they saw the largest canoe they had ever seen. Not only was it long, it was also beamed, with a cabin below for passengers. It was carrying cotton cloth, copper items, pots for melting ore like copper, fruit, beer, and cacao beans. The beans were used like money. The captain of the canoe explained that they were from the mainland and were on a trading voyage in the islands. Columbus realized that the man, being a trader, was good at communicating and ordered the man, whom he named Juan Perez, to stay with his fleet as guide and interpreter.

Then the fleet headed for Cape Honduras on the north of the island. They anchored there and took on fresh water and provisions. Meanwhile, Columbus tried to figure out just where to begin looking for the strait for which he was searching. He decided to go east, even though he knew it would be harder sailing than if he were to go west.

It took them nearly a month battling against rain and storms to round the northern part of Honduras. Columbus later wrote that he had never seen so long a storm:

> *What griped me most were the sufferings of my son; to think that so young a lad, only thirteen, should go through so much. But our Lord lent him such courage that he even heartened the rest, and he worked as though he had been to sea all of a long life. That comforted me. I was sick and many times lay at death's door, but gave orders from a doghouse that the people clapped together for me on the poop deck. My brother was in the worst of the ships, the crank one, and I felt terribly having persuaded him to come against his will.*

Rounding the cape, they came upon Nicaragua, and further on, Costa Rica. Columbus formally took possession of these lands for Spain, but he found nothing of great interest. The Talamanca Indians had more *guanin*, the combination of gold and copper, but the *guanin* that Columbus had sent back before had made no big hit in Spain, so he didn't want to be bothered with it. They did find some interesting animals, including a spider monkey.

Further along, they found people wearing gold ornaments and were able to trade hawks' bells and glass beads for them. On October 5, Columbus thought he had at last found the strait he was searching for. Unfortunately he had let the captured interpreter go home by that time, so it was hard to communicate with the Indians. He spread his arms wide in a sign for ocean, but they thought he just meant a large body of water and directed him to a lagoon.

It did not take Columbus long to find out that he was in a lagoon. From the Indians who came out to trade with the ships, he learned that they were near a spot where the land narrowed between two seas. But they also told him that the narrow spot was marked by mountain ranges. Had Columbus tried to cross this narrow bit of land, later to be called the Isthmus of Panama, he would have seen the Pacific Ocean. But he did not make that attempt. In fact, he gave up his search for a strait.

While in that lagoon, he had found something that interested him as much, if not more than his quest for a strait: gold. The Guaymi Indians wore gold ornaments and were quite happy to trade them for hawks' bells and beads. Columbus started thinking about setting up another trading post.

The four ships set sail again on October 17, 1502, staying near the coast of Panama, looking for a place to start a settlement. There were few harbors, but those at which the fleet did stop were not what Columbus wanted, for one reason or another. Mainly, it was because the Indians had no gold. These included the beautiful harbor that Columbus named Puerto Bello (Beautiful Port). This was very close to the Isthmus of Panama. But Columbus decided to keep looking.

By early December, Columbus had decided that

the best chance for finding gold lay back where they had come from. So, he ordered the fleet to turn around. By the time they reached Puerto Bello, the weather had turned rough. It rained for days and days, and the winds buffeted the small ships back and forth. At one point, the ships were separated, although they found one another a couple of days later. Everyone aboard was tired and weary of the bad weather. They were also weak with hunger, for the ships' supplies were dangerously low. Ferdinand later wrote that the hardtack that was left was so full of small beetles called weevils that, hungry as they were, some of the men waited until darkness to eat. That way, they didn't have to see what they were eating.

While weevils were infesting the food supplies, *teredos* were doing the same thing to the bottoms of the ships. These shipworms burrowed holes in the hulls of ships and eventually could cause a ship's bottom to drop out completely. Before setting out on the voyage, the ships' hulls had been thoroughly scraped and coated with pitch. But the *teredos* seemed to like the pitch as much as the wood. When the fleet pulled into the Panamanian harbor, now called Coco Solo, on December 23, Columbus ordered the hull of the *Gallega* cleaned (the process is called *careening* because it is necessary to tilt the ship on its side).

Shortly after New Year's Day, 1503, the fleet set off to the west again and on January 6 anchored off the mouth of a river that Columbus named Belén. He chose the Spanish word for Bethlehem because January 6 was the day of the Feast of Three Kings, who had brought gifts to the Christ Child in Bethlehem. Perhaps because he thought it was an omen that they had found a place to anchor on that day, Columbus decided to build his trading post there.

10
Marooned

It wasn't long before Columbus learned that he had chosen one of the wettest sites in Panama for his trading post. It rains so much there that the ground is constantly saturated with water, and any new rainfall can cause floods. Late in January there was a rainstorm in the mountains above the mouth of the Belén, and a torrent of water came crashing down upon the ships. It was so strong that it caused the *Capitana* to drag on her anchor and bump into the *Gallega*.

Meanwhile, however, Bartholomew had taken an expedition up the next river, the Veragua, and made contact with the local *cacique*, whose name was Quibian. Quibian gave the party guides, who took the men to a place where they were able to dig up large quantities of gold grains with just their pocket knives. This was enough to cause Columbus to start building his trading post, which he named Santa María de Belén.

But soon there was trouble with the inhabitants. Some of the Spaniards decided to invade Indian villages in search of women and gold. Quibian realized that the strangers were building their own fort and thatched huts and figured that the raids would only continue if he didn't do something. He started sending groups of his men in canoes down the Belén. Columbus had a feeling that their mission was to find the best place for an attack.

It was then that Diego Méndez began to show his value to Columbus and others aboard the Spanish ships. He volunteered to find out what was going on. In a rowboat, he went along the coast until he came upon a large encampment of warriors obviously preparing for battle. Instead of quickly returning to Santa María de Belén, he actually went ashore and told the Indians that he knew what they were planning. Then he went back to the boat and spent the night watching the camp.

Now that the Spaniards knew about their plan, the warriors were not sure what to do. So, they returned to Quibian's village. Méndez went back to the trading post to tell Columbus what he had seen. Then, he set off again for Quibian's village. He found the villagers preparing for war, and once again he confronted the warriors. This time, though, he did a strange thing. He took out scissors and had another man with him cut his hair. The Indians were so curious about what was going on that they stopped their war dancing. Quibian was so intrigued that he had his hair cut, too. Méndez gave him a present of a comb, scissors, and a mirror.

When Méndez reported to Columbus that he had found the Indians again preparing for war, Columbus decided to capture Quibian. Méndez led the force that seized the *cacique* and his family and brought them back to Santa María de Belén. Unfortunately for Columbus, Quibian escaped and quickly raised another force to attack the European settlement.

Meanwhile, the Belén river had fallen so low that a sandbar now prevented the four ships from going back out to sea. The sailors managed to tow three of the ships across the bar. Columbus ordered that the fourth, the *Gallega,* remain on the other side. She could be used as a floating fort. His plan was to leave Bartholomew and a small force behind at Santa María de Belén while he and the rest returned to Spain for more ships, supplies, and men.

The three ships were about to get under way when a force of four hundred Indians attacked the fort. Bartholomew and about twenty men, plus the Irish wolfhound, managed to beat them off. But in retreat the Indians came upon Diego Tristan, captain of the *Capitana.* He and about ten men were upriver loading up with fresh water. The Indians killed all but one of the Spaniards.

Now, Bartholomew decided that he did not want to be left behind at Santa María de Belén, surrounded by angry Indians. Columbus agreed that it would not be wise to risk the lives of his brother and the other men. Now the problem was how to get them and their supplies across the sandbar. Once again, Diego Méndez stepped in. He built a raft on which they floated across the bar to the ships on the other side. They had to abandon the *Gallega.* Columbus never returned to Santa María de Belén.

Columbus decided it was time to return home. But they needed supplies. They also needed to careen the ships, for the busy shipworms were doing great damage to the hulls. So, they would go first to Santo Domingo. He was quite sure that meant sailing eastward until they were at a point due south of Hispaniola. The pilots with him disagreed. They reckoned that they were already due south of Hispaniola. But Columbus insisted that he was right.

It was slow going. The strong easterly winds hindered them, and the ships' hulls were so badly damaged that the sailors had to spend day and night pumping and bailing out the water seeping into the holds. Soon, no amount of pumping and bailing could save the *Vizcaina.* She had to be abandoned and her crew divided between the two remaining ships, the *Capitana* and the *Bermuda.* This did nothing to improve the mood of the crew.

In early May, the pilots insisted that the two-ship fleet head northward at once. Columbus was ill with malaria, suffering from arthritis, and in despair over the failure of Santa María de Belén. He gave in to their demands. The ships turned

110

northward, battling the currents and thunderstorms. Two weeks later they reached Cuba, which proved that the pilots had been wrong about their location. But Columbus was in no mood to say "I told you so." He had to concentrate all his energies on getting the ships to Santo Domingo.

He could have proceeded along the Cuban coast and then crossed the Windward Passage to Hispaniola. But he was afraid the ships would not hold up that long. Instead, he decided to head for open sea, hoping the swift currents that would carry them east to Hispaniola would not prove too strong for the leaky hulls. But about one hundred miles away from Hispaniola, the *Bermuda* began to take on so much water that she was in danger of sinking. Columbus set a course for Jamaica where the ships could take refuge.

The ships entered a bay that Columbus had named Santa Gloria on his second voyage (today it is called St. Ann's Bay). He ordered them to run aground. His men pushed sand up under their keels so they would not tip. Then, they set about gathering palm stalks and fronds to build thatched huts on the decks. These would be their homes until they could get help. They had no idea how long that would be.

The local Indians were friendly. Columbus decided to keep them that way by not allowing his men to go ashore. He knew very well that if allowed ashore the men would soon be stealing women and causing the friendly Indians to turn unfriendly fast. More than anything else, the marooned Europeans needed the help of local people, because they needed food.

For their entire time at Santa Gloria, Columbus and his men depended completely on the local inhabitants for their food. If they went fishing or hunting, it was more for sport than to feed themselves. Historians don't know exactly why, since no one in Santa Gloria ever explained it. The reason may have been that many of the sailors were young and had no experience fishing and hunting. More likely, the reason was that the Europeans did not consider it appropriate to get their own food. They considered it their right to have other people do it for them.

A century and a half later, the Dutch colonists in New Amsterdam (present-day New York) depended entirely on the Indians for the game that they ate. If the Indians didn't hunt for deer, the Dutch colonists had no deer meat to eat. The Dutch colonists had guns, but they did not hunt game with them. If there had been no Indians around New Amsterdam, the Dutch colonists would have had to hunt for themselves. But as long as there were Indians, the Indians did the hunting.

The same was probably true of Columbus and his men at Santa Gloria. If they had been marooned on a deserted island, they would have figured out how to hunt and fish for their food. But there were Indians to do that work for them.

Columbus sent Diego Méndez and a small party ashore to find food. They bought food from the natives and a canoe to carry it. Then Méndez drew up a written agreement with the Indians. It set forth the prices the Europeans were willing to pay for food: a cake of cassava bread was worth two glass beads, a large quantity of fish was worth one hawk's bell, and so on.

Once Columbus, with the help of Méndez, had taken care of the immediate needs of his men for shelter and food, he turned his attention to the bigger problem of how to get them out of Santa Gloria. He made no plans to build a ship from the timbers of the two grounded vessels. The reason may have been that his sailors were too young to know how to build a ship. He had little hope that any Spanish vessel would happen to pass by, since he had already reported that there was no gold on Jamaica. His only hope was to get a message to Santo Domingo.

The logical person to send was Diego Méndez, who had come through for the expedition in so many other crises. Méndez ordered that the dugout canoe he had bought from the Indians be fixed up with a mast and sail and keel. The canoe was loaded with provisions, and Columbus entrusted Méndez with a report on the voyage to be sent back to Spain from Hispaniola. Then Méndez set out for Hispaniola, traveling along the shore of Jamaica until he reached what they called the Northeast Point. But somewhere around the Northeast Point he was captured by Indians. He escaped and managed to get back to Santa Gloria.

He tried again the next day. This time, there were two canoes in the expedition, the other one piloted by Captain Bartolomeo Fieschi, a Genoese. Each canoe had six Spanish sailors and ten Indians, whose job was to do the paddling and the other work under the direction of the Europeans. Bartholomew Columbus provided an armed escort in other dugouts bought from the Indians. The armed escort saw the two "sailing canoes" safely to the Northeast Point and watched them set off across the Windward Passage toward Hispaniola.

This was a bold adventure indeed. What was called a small-boat journey had never before been tried by Europeans in these waters. The Europeans were not used to such a voyage, nor were the Indians. It is said that several Indians died because they drank up their water rations too soon. Others died when the two sailing canoes reached Navassa Island and everyone had fresh water to drink; the Indians drank too much of it at one time. Perhaps the reason why the Indians drank their water so quickly was that they worked harder and needed it more. In any event, all the Europeans were alive when the canoes reached Hispaniola about four days after they left Jamaica.

Governor Ovando was in no hurry to save Christopher Columbus. In fact, he kept putting off Diego Méndez, who was ordered to stay in the interior of Hispaniola, away from Santo Domingo. Between August, 1503, and March, 1504, Ovando did not send a rescue mission to Jamaica or authorize Méndez to do so. Finally, in March, he let Méndez go to Santo Domingo to try to hire a rescue ship.

Meanwhile, all Columbus and the other marooned Europeans on Jamaica could do was wait. They did not know if Méndez had reached Hispaniola or perished at sea. For many of the men, the wait was too long. On New Year's Day, 1504, about half the marooned men mutinied under the leadership of the Porras brothers.

The Porras brothers had taken part in the expedition because the Treasurer of Castile had wanted them to. They were not loyal to Columbus. During the long months of waiting at Santa Gloria, they had complained often and loudly that Columbus really didn't want to go to Hispaniola. After all, he was doing nothing to get them there. They had been waiting too long. Diego Méndez must have been lost at sea. The thing to do was to take some dugouts and make another attempt to reach the Spanish colony.

Columbus was in no danger during this mutiny. The Porras brothers and their followers simply left the two grounded ships and set off on their own in ten canoes. As they made their way east along the coast of Jamaica, they robbed any Indians they could find and took a number of Indians captive to serve as paddlers. Reaching the Northeast Point, they set out to sea. But the winds soon drove them back. Deciding that they were carrying too great a load, they threw most of their supplies, and most of the Indians, into the sea and tried again. But again they were unsuccessful in fighting the winds. After still another attempt, they abandoned the canoes. They decided to make it alone on Jamaica and wait for a time when they could ambush Columbus and his men at Santa Gloria and maybe capture one of the ships to sail on.

Meanwhile, food supplies at Santa Gloria were dangerously low, even without the forty-eight or so mutineers who had left. The Indians had all the hawks' bells and beads they could use and had no reason to keep feeding the marooned Europeans. So, Columbus resorted to clever trickery. From his 1504 almanac he knew that a total eclipse of the moon was due on the last night of February, 1504. He told the Indians that God wanted them to provide food. God was unhappy that the Indians were not supplying food and would soon show how unhappy He was. Columbus told the Indians to watch the moon that night to see what he was talking about.

That night, just as the almanac had predicted, the earth was in a position exactly between the sun and the moon, blocking out all light from the sun and seeming to cover up the moon completely. The Indians were terribly frightened. They begged Columbus to stop it. Columbus stayed in his cabin until he knew that the eclipse was about over. Then he emerged and announced that he had asked God to stop it, provided that the Indians continued to bring him and his men food. Sure enough, the eclipse ended. From then on, the Indians brought all the food that was needed.

A ship sailed into the Santa Gloria harbor at the end of March, 1504. At first, Columbus and the marooned sailors thought they were about to be rescued. But Governor Ovando had sent the ship only to see if Columbus was still alive. Its captain had strict orders not to take on any passengers. The captain brought a message from Méndez that he had made it to Santo Domingo and was trying to charter a rescue ship. He also ordered his men to unload a couple of barrels of wine and a side of salt pork for the marooned men. Then, the ship took off again, leaving the marooned men in almost total despair.

Still, the message from Méndez had given Columbus hope. He was certain that they would eventually be rescued. He decided to put the affairs of Santa Gloria in order before that happened, which meant making peace with the Porras brothers and their band of mutineers who were still hiding somewhere nearby. But the Porras brothers saw his advances as a sign of weakness. They led an attack on Santa Gloria. The Columbus brothers and their loyal forces beat them back and forced the surrender of the mutineers. Everyone but the Porras brothers was pardoned. The brothers were placed under guard on shore.

Finally in late June, 1504, Diego Méndez arrived in a small, leaky ship from Santo Domingo. The approximately one hundred marooned men, plus supplies, so overloaded the little ship that she practically sank on the way back. All hands worked the pumps day and night to keep her afloat. But after a slow, frightening journey of more than six weeks, she anchored at Santo Domingo. After more than a year, the marooned men were saved. Later, when both were back in Spain, Columbus told Méndez that he had never in his life known so joyful a day, for he had not expected to leave that place alive.

Columbus had no wish to remain in Santo Domingo any longer than was necessary. But he did have some business to conduct with Ovando. Namely, to get the gold that was owed him as Viceroy of the Indies. Ovando turned over to him a chest of gold to take home. In addition, Columbus claimed more gold, worth about $180,000, and put his mark on it, ordering Ovando to send it to him in Spain. As soon as he could, Columbus hired a ship back to Spain. Only twenty-three others from his original expedition went back with him. The rest could not face another voyage and stayed at Santo Domingo. The voyage home was long and difficult because of bad weather, but at last, on November 7, 1504, the ship reached Spain.

As long as he lived after that, and it wasn't long, Christopher Columbus referred to his fourth voyage to the Indies as *El Alto Viaje*, the High Voyage. It certainly had been full of adventure! But it just about did in the long-suffering men who were part of it. Ferdinand Columbus never went to sea again. Nor did his father. We do not know about the others.

11
End of a Journey

By the time Columbus reached Spain in early November, 1504, Queen Isabella was gravely ill. Columbus waited at Seville for a summons to court, but that summons did not come. Since it was customary for nearly all captains who had gone on overseas voyages to report to the king and queen on their return, Columbus had to suspect that the royal couple didn't want to see him.

It was probably King Ferdinand who made the decision not to invite Columbus to court. He had received the report that Columbus had sent by way of Diego Méndez when Méndez set off for Hispaniola. By most accounts, it was not very convincing. In the report, Columbus had been very defensive about the difficulties he'd had, spending too much time explaining why he'd had such problems. He had also gone on too long with so-called proofs that he had been sailing in the Far East. Ferdinand may have decided that he didn't want to listen to more of this from Columbus in person.

Isabella died in late November. Columbus would have liked to have gone to the funeral, along with everyone else who thought it might bring them some favor with the court. But Columbus was suffering from severe arthritis and was too ill to travel. All he could do was write to his sons and ask them to do what they could on his behalf.

Their father's problems had not affected the standing of Diego and Ferdinand at court. Twenty-four-year-old Diego was now a member of the royal bodyguard. Sixteen-year-old Ferdinand had been able to return to his position as a page and had also been given his full pay for the voyage with his father.

Others on that voyage were not so lucky. Columbus spent a great deal of time writing letters to the Treasurer of Castile asking him to pay the seamen and officers. But they did not get their money for more than two years of service until several years later.

Columbus did not have to worry about money for himself. He had the chest of gold he had brought back and the gold that had come through on the *Aguja*, the one ship from Ovando's thirty-ship fleet that had survived the hurricane intact. But money concerned him nevertheless. Once he had been denied the power he had expected to have over Hispaniola and the other islands of the

Indies that he had discovered, he became greatly concerned with at least getting the wealth that had been promised him. He wrote many letters to Diego at court, asking his son to confirm his rights to various percentages of gold and pearls and the other wealth from the Indies.

He was not after this for himself, but rather to finance yet another voyage to the Other World. He realized that at fifty-three and as ill as he was, he would not be able to make that voyage himself. Instead, he wanted Diego to go. He also wanted King Ferdinand to make Diego viceroy after he died. Diego was willing to go along with his father's wishes. He made his relationship with the king more solid by marrying a lady of royal blood named Doña María de Toledo. Diego's bride was the niece of one of the king's cousins.

As the months wore on, it became more and more important to Columbus that his titles be confirmed by the king, and that the king also confirm the original agreement that these titles would pass to his heirs after he died. He swallowed his pride over not being invited to court and decided to ask to be heard. By this time, the spring of 1505, he felt well enough to travel.

Now, the only problem was that he did not feel well enough to travel by horse. He needed the slower pace of a mule ride. But to ride a mule to court he had to obtain special permission from King Ferdinand. It seems that breeders of horses had persuaded the king to pass a law against using mules for riding. The king gave his permission, and Columbus became one of the only men in Spain with the right to ride a mule.

In May, 1505, Ferdinand, and thus the Spanish court, was at Segovia, north of Madrid. It was a long journey from Seville, especially by slow mule ride, but Columbus was determined to make it, no matter how tired and stiff he became. King Ferdinand received him in a friendly manner. But the king suggested that an arbitrator be appointed — someone who was not involved in the matter, to study his claims against the Crown. These claims, according to the king, included not just money but also the titles of admiral and viceroy. Columbus disagreed. He had no intention of letting an arbitrator decide on whether or not he should have the titles he believed were rightfully his.

The matter was still unresolved when the king left Segovia for Salamanca. So, Columbus followed the court. When the court moved to Valladolid, Columbus once again followed. He spent a year waiting and moving to other places to wait. Meanwhile, all this travel, even on mule-back, was doing his health no good.

Columbus felt that he would die soon. He sent letters to his family, asking them to join him. He also made his will. When Bartholomew arrived, Christopher sent his brother to court on his behalf. Bartholomew was at court when Columbus died on May 20, 1506.

Both sons, Diego and Ferdinand, were with Columbus during his last days. So was his younger brother, Diego, and a few loyal followers, including Diego Méndez and Bartolomeo Fieschi. A priest said Mass and gave him the last rites. Columbus's last words were the same ones that Jesus said as he died on the cross: "Into Thy hands, O Lord, I commit my spirit." His faith in God was still as strong as ever.

Christopher Columbus, Admiral of the Ocean Sea, Viceroy and Governor of the Islands and Mainlands in the Indies, had a simple funeral. Very few people mourned the passing of the man who had discovered new lands and new ocean routes to the West. King Ferdinand did honor his wishes by naming Diego Governor of Hispaniola and giving him the other honorary titles that Columbus had held.

In 1508 Diego was named Governor of the Indies, and in 1509 he went to Santo Domingo to take up his post. Two years later, he was made Viceroy of the Islands, but no mention was made of the mainland. He made several voyages to Spain to try to persuade the court to give him governing power over the mainland as well. He was in Spain in 1526 when he died. His son, Luis, settled with the Spanish Crown. In return for the title of Admiral of the Indies, the island of Jamaica, an estate on the Isthmus of Panama, and a yearly sum of money, he gave up all other claims in the New World.

Christopher Columbus died never knowing that he had come nowhere near the Far East. It wasn't until Ferdinand Magellan, a Portuguese navigator sailing for the Spanish Crown, crossed the Strait of Magellan, that Europeans realized there was another ocean. Magellan set out from Spain with five ships on September 20, 1519, entered the strait that today bears his name on October 21, 1520, and reached the Pacific on November 28, 1520. He continued west but was killed in 1521 in the Philippines while supporting one warring local group against the other. The other ships, which numbered only three by this time, continued on. Eventually, the lone ship *Victoria*, commanded by Juan Sebastian del Cano, went all the way around the world. The *Victoria* landed back in Spain on September 22, 1522, three years almost to the day when the original five ships had set out on the expedition.

By the time the sole survivor of Magellan's fleet completed the first known trip in recorded history around the world and proved that Columbus's "Indies" were nowhere near the real Indies, it was too late for the native peoples whom Columbus had called Indians. Not only were they stuck with a name that was not theirs, but most of them were dead.

Natives of what later came to be called the West Indies suffered terribly under the Spanish. Forced to work as slaves to cultivate fields and mine gold, and exposed to European diseases, they died in huge numbers. There is no way of knowing how many Lucayan were living in the islands around Samana Cay when Columbus made his first landfall there and named it San Salvador. It is known that within forty years — some say as early as 1513 — not a single Lucayan was left. No people live on that island to this day. Peoples in other parts of the West Indies and in Central America did not fare much better. It is difficult to guess how many of the natives died because of slavery and how many died because they had no immunity to European diseases.

Christopher Columbus wrote and talked about discovering an Other World to the west. But it was Amerigo Vespucci whose name was given to that world. Vespucci was the young Florentine sailor who had sailed to Paria to search for pearls in 1498 with Alonso de Ojeda. He later wrote an account of the voyage, which was probably accurate in most respects. But according to some historians there was one big error: He said the voyage had occurred in 1496 instead of 1498–99.

Later on, Amerigo Vespucci made voyages of his own to South America. In 1508, he was named Chief Pilot of Spain.

Columbus had called the new continent and the islands he had discovered an Other World. Vespucci called them a New World. Vespucci's name stuck. It was picked up by a monk of German heritage named Martin Waldseemuller. In 1507, Waldseemuller drew a map of the world that showed all the new discoveries. He included the new continent that we know as South America and named it America after Amerigo Vespucci. Others picked up that name from his map, where it was first used.

The name of Columbus may not be on a continent or continents, but the names he gave to many islands and some groups of islands remain the same today. The West Indies islands got their overall name because he originally thought they were the East Indies. The Virgin Islands are so named because he named them after the "11,000 virgins" of legend. Individual islands like Guadaloupe, Trinidad, and Hispaniola still carry the names Columbus gave them.

Epilogue

While no continent was named after Columbus, a large number of other things bear his name. There is a port called Colombo in Sri Lanka on the Indian Ocean, although Columbus never sailed anywhere near there. There is a Columbus Archipelago (the Galápagos Islands) near Ecuador in South America, although Columbus never got there, either. In South America, there is the nation of Colombia. In North America, there are cities and towns named Columbus in Georgia, Illinois, Indiana, Iowa, Kansas, Kentucky, Mississippi, Montana, Nebraska, New Mexico, North Carolina, Ohio, South Dakota, Texas, and Wisconsin. There are also towns named Columbia, such as in Maryland. Our nation's capital of Washington, D.C., is located in the District of Columbia.

There is a Columbus Avenue and a Columbia University in New York City. One of the nicknames of the American flag (besides Old Glory) is Columbia.

With all these Columbuses and Columbias in the United States, you'd think that Christopher Columbus landed on Plymouth Rock! Many people who haven't read much of history are under the incorrect impression that he landed somewhere on North American shores, because we Americans have managed over the years to adopt him as our own.

It's hard to tell exactly how this happened, but there was something about this brave and adventurous sailor that appealed to Americans, and so, over time, Columbus became "Americanized." The Americanization of Columbus began after the thirteen colonies won their independence from Great Britain and declared themselves the United States of America. A brand-new country needed new heroes and new symbols. George Washington, the first president, was regarded almost as a king. Christopher Columbus seemed like another important symbol of adventure, independence, individuality, and courage in facing the unknown. The two men somehow became connected in the American mind. Thus, when the new Congress decided on a capital of the new nation in 1790, the congressmen agreed to call it Washington. They also agreed to carve out of Maryland a special federal district, which in 1791 they decided to call the District of Columbia.

Just a few years earlier, in 1784, Kings College in New York City reorganized under the new name Columbia University.

The first Columbus Day celebration was held in New York City in 1792, although it didn't attract a great deal of interest. In Washington, D.C., a monument to Columbus was built in front of the U.S. capitol during the middle of the nineteenth century.

In the late nineteenth century, the United States celebrated two centennials. One was the 100th anniversary of independence in 1876. Another was the 100th anniversary of the inauguration of George Washington. By 1892, Americans were ready for another celebration, this time of the 400th anniversary of Columbus's landing in the New World in 1492. President Benjamin Harrison issued a proclamation urging schools to have programs and special festivals honoring Columbus. In Chicago, a great world's fair was planned to celebrate the anniversary and was called the "World's Columbian Exposition." Unfortunately, it took the planners longer than expected to get the fair ready, and the gates did not open until the summer of 1893. On October 12, 1893, the fair was the setting for the most elaborate celebration of Columbus's discovery ever held in the United States. The pledge of allegiance to the flag was written to mark the 400th anniversary of Christopher Columbus's first voyage to the New World. Composed by a Baptist minister named Francis Bellamy, it first appeared in a magazine for young people called *The Youth's Companion* in 1892.

Columbus Day celebrations began to be held widely in the first years of the twentieth century. The Knights of Columbus, an organization of Catholic men, urged that October 12 be a holiday in many states, and beginning in 1905, with Colorado, several states began to celebrate the day. In 1909, New York became the first state to declare October 12 a state holiday. Other states followed, although some called it Discovery Day and Landing Day. In 1968 President Lyndon B. Johnson signed a law that would make Columbus Day a federal holiday. The law went into effect in 1971.

In the mid-twentieth century a group of Native Americans was successful in getting the Columbus monument removed from in front of the U.S. capitol. They pointed out that their ancestors were already in the Americas when Columbus arrived, that Columbus had mis-named them by calling them Indians, and that Columbus had been the first European to enslave Native Americans. They were successful in their campaign and the monument was removed.

Almost all nations in the western hemisphere celebrate Columbus's voyage. In Central and South America the observances are more religious than they are in the United States.

Today, Christopher Columbus is still considered very much a part of American life. One of the space shuttles is named *Columbia*. If Columbus were alive today, he would be astonished at how much he is celebrated. He would probably be very pleased, but he would be careful not to be too pleased, not wanting to commit the sin of pride.

For Further Reading

Bradford, Ernle. *Christopher Columbus*. New York: Viking Press, 1973.

Bradley, Michael. *The Black Discovery of America*. Toronto: Personal Library, 1981.

Deagan, Kathleen A. "Searching for Columbus's Lost Colony." *National Geographic*, vol. 172, no. 5 (November 1987), pp. 672–675.

Judge, Joseph. "Where Columbus Found the New World." *National Geographic*, vol. 170, no. 5 (November 1986), pp. 567–572; 578–599.

Leon, George DeLucenay. *Explorers of the Americas Before Columbus*. New York: Franklin Watts, 1989.

Lyon, Eugene. "15th-Century Manuscript Yields First Look at *Niña*." *National Geographic*, vol. 170, no. 5 (November 1986), pp. 601–605.

Marden, Luis. "The First Landfall of Columbus." *National Geographic*, vol. 170, no. 5 (November 1986), pp. 572–577.

Morison, Samuel Eliot. *Christopher Columbus, Mariner*. Boston: Little, Brown, 1942.

Soule, Gardner. *Christopher Columbus on the Green Sea of Darkness*. New York: Franklin Watts, 1988.

Van Sertima, Ivan. *They Came Before Columbus*. New York: Random House, 1976.

Index

135

I

J

K

L

M

N